GLORY IN THE CENTRE SPOT

Eric Ashton

GLORY IN THE
CENTRE SPOT

Scratching Shed Publishing Ltd

Rugby League Classics

This edition published by Scratching Shed Publishing Ltd, 2009
Registered in England & Wales No. 6588772.
Registered office:
47 Street Lane, Leeds, West Yorkshire. LS8 1AP

www.scratchingshedpublishing.co.uk

Cover image: Eric Ashton leads his Wigan team down the steps at
Wembley after beating Hull 30-13 in the 1959 Challenge Cup Final
Picture by kind courtesy of Rugby League Journal

Back page photo: *Seated left to right* - Brian McTigue, Eric Ashton
& Billy Boston show off the Challenge Cup

Glory In The Centre Spot was originally published by Pelham Books,
Bloomsbury, London, in 1966

A catalogue record for this book is available from the British Library.

ISBN 978-0956007544

Typeset in Warnock Pro Semi Bold and Palatino

Printed and bound in the United Kingdom by
L.P.P.S.Ltd, Wellingborough, Northants, NN8 3PJ

Rugby League Classics

Glory In The Centre Spot is the third in a fascinating series of historically significant Rugby League Classics, rescued, rebranded and re-issued in paperback, often after being long out-of-print. Each edition comes complete with the original manuscript intact and contains a wealth of new and updated material, including an introductory overview written by a relevant modern-day expert, evocative photographs, appendices, and the recollections of those closest to the book's primary subject, i.e. family members, former team-mates and other contemporary figures.

In order to stay as true to the spirit of the original text as possible, all editing has purposely been kept to a minimum. Readers should be aware, therefore, that although factual inaccuracies by the original writer - should they occur - may be referred to and corrected in the new introduction, in the main text they will be allowed to stand. In the interests of readability, however, occasional errors in spelling and grammar (which may well have frustrated the author at the time) have now been amended, along with inconsistencies in house style and the odd distracting archaism.

Scratching Shed Publishing Ltd

Scratching Shed Publishing Limited is an independent publishing company founded in May 2008. We aim to produce high-quality books covering a wide range of subjects, including sport, travel and popular culture, that are of interest to the world, yet which offer a distinctive flavour of the North of England.

Acknowledgements

The publishers of *Glory In The Centre Spot* are grateful to a number of people who helped to make the updating and re-publication of this autobiography possible.

Most obviously, our thanks go to Eric Ashton's charming wife, Doreen, who along with her daughters, Michelle and Beverley, gave the project her support from the start.

Our gratitude, too, to a couple of Eric's life-long friends and colleagues. Ray French propped up the front row, writing an excellent introduction and providing invaluable support throughout. Fulfiling a similar role at the back, meanwhile, is that linchpin of any history involving the St. Helens club, Denis Whittle. Denis kindly gave us his own personal tribute to Eric, a copy of Eric's 1969 Testimonial programme - reprinted in full from page 179 - and several wonderful photographs.

The ever-reliable Mike Latham compiled Eric's career statistics, while Harry Edgar's splendid *Rugby League Journal* was another invaluable source of photography; the finest example of which graces the front cover of this new edition.

In giving us permission to reprint an article from Dave Hadfield's 'Icons of League' series, originally published in *Rugby League World* magazine in May 2008, Mr Hadfield and League Publications Ltd were especially helpful.

And finally, a sincere thank you to Leslie Smith and his team at the highly recommended National Archive of Rugby League Video Interviews, whose admirable enterprise enabled us to continue Eric Ashton's story where *Glory In The Centre Spot* left off.

Contents

INTRODUCTION

by Ray French
**Dual-code England rugby international and
rugby league commentator on BBC television and radio**

It is widely and quite rightly believed that the Wigan and Great Britain wing pairing of Eric Ashton and Billy Boston was one of the most effective attacking partnerships ever seen in the history of rugby league. The amount of tries scored and the sheer number of matches won in the 'fifties and 'sixties by their uncanny, telepathic understanding more than bears testament to that. And yet the very first wing partner for Eric, the legendary Wigan centre and RFL Hall of Fame member, was not dashing, barnstorming Billy Boston from Cardiff. It was yours truly; Ray French.

Yes, as an eleven-year-old, I made my rugby debut outside Eric on the Congregational Church field which, in those days, nestled in the shadow of the St. Helens RL club's Knowsley Road ground. The occasion was a match between a MacFarlane Avenue-Fairclough Road team and an Ellison Drive-Mulberry Avenue select. Twenty-five players per side under touch rugby rules and with no referee. Happy days, and what an apprenticeship for professional rugby league.

On most weeknights during the summer and after Sunday School on the Sabbath, forty to fifty youngsters from our district, aged between ten and sixteen, met on the local field to play a touch rugby match that could last upwards of four to five hours, with a large, misshapen and worn-out leather ball. Lads left and returned to the game at regular intervals, as and when their mothers, often perched high on the surrounding wooden fence, called them in for their dinner or tea. Ten-year-old novices played alongside strapping talented teenagers and were expected to come up to scratch too, or else be banished to the wing where, as a result of the enormous number of players on either side, the ball seldom reached. The only fate worse was the one meted out to the very poorest young offenders. These unfortunates were expected to stand with their arms above their head and act as goalposts, whenever a conversion was attempted.

My own role, thankfully, was to be one of half-a-dozen wingers to a fifteen-year-old Eric Ashton, but I was certainly never expected to perform it with anything like the aplomb that Billy Boston later did. Nor could I ever aspire to scoring over 478 tries, a feat that the powerful Welshman achieved while playing for Wigan outside our mutual St. Helens-born centre. Billy, on the other hand, whether in action alongside Eric at Central Park, London's Wembley Stadium or the Sydney Cricket Ground, was never made to search for the ball in the long grass, whenever it rolled over the touchline. Nor was he told to climb the wire netting which surrounded the tennis courts, whenever the ball was kicked over there. A different set of skills entirely, you see. But I have no doubt that, back in the 'forties and 'fifties, such games on humble patches of grass like the Congregational Church field played a huge part in helping to develop the skills and attitudes that would, one day, allow countless youngsters to become international rugby players.

Eric Ashton certainly served his apprenticeship in such surroundings. When teams of twenty-five plus players are battling each other under touch rugby rules then speed of thought, instant decision making and precision passing of the ball via the fingertips are required if the player in possession is not to be touched, and thereby bring about the end of the movement. In touch rugby there can be no place for selfishness and there is no way that size alone can allow someone to brush aside or burst through a would-be tackler if the movement can be stopped by an opponent simply laying a hand on any part of the attacker's body. Instead, there is a need for clever footwork, speed and, especially, a quick change of gear in order to confuse a covering defence.

Above all, one must always be aware of a player who is in a better position than you. An eleven-year-old marking a fifteen or even sixteen-year-old could never lack courage and, with ball in hand, he needed a belief in his own abilities too - there were most likely bigger and older team-mates crying out for you to give them the ball. On top of that, older boys were able to gather the maturity that allowed them to organise play and order younger team members around.

Yes, the experience of that Congregational Church field and our seemingly endless hours playing upon it were invaluable to myself and others who later carved successful rugby league and rugby union careers. And they were plainly instrumental in moulding Eric Ashton into the type of player that he was destined to become - quite simply one of the finest leaders that the thirteen-a-side code has ever seen, and a true rugby league legend worldwide.

Like all good touch rugby players, then, Eric was blessed not just with pace, but with the ability to vary that pace at will, along with an uncanny sense of when to pass or not to pass to a player alongside him. He had a knack for finding gaps in the tightest of defences and an eye for searching out weakness in an opposing side; a quality that enabled him and his team to dictate terms to, and instill fear in, those who were lined up against them. His self-confidence and instinct for leadership lifted him above every other captain of his generation, inspiring those who played under him to produce often quite extraordinary performances, whether at club or international level. Eric was utterly selfless in his play and many are the players who owe their days or moments of glory to one of his shrewd passes, precision kicks or instructive shouts, when a game was at its most intense and the result was truly in doubt. Eric was one of the most gifted players in rugby league history, a masterful tactician and inspirational general. For those of us who were lucky enough to watch him in action or play alongside him, it is obvious why Eric attained such distinction, not only as a player but as a coach and a chairman.

This introduction has been no exception to the rule which states that whenever the name Eric Ashton occurs in conversation or print, it is usually accompanied by that of Billy Boston, such was - and is - the fame of their wing partnership in the famous cherry and white jersey of Wigan, or red, white and blue of Great Britain. But the name of Eric Ashton can and should stand alone, for his achievements in rugby league and for the excitement and entertainment his individual skills provided for the sport's hundreds of thousands of fans on both ends of the planet.

As the man himself reveals in his autobiography, within months of being, ironically, rejected by his home town club, St. Helens, Eric, whilst undergoing National Army Service, was playing in the first team of Saints' deadly local rivals Wigan, to whom he had signed for a mere £150. He didn't know it then, of course, but he was on the road to playing over 497 matches for Wigan in a glittering career that began in 1955 and ended in 1969, some three years after the publication of 'Glory In The Centre Spot'. During that time, he amassed over 1,589 points, from 231 tries and 448 goals. His points-scoring tally is indicative of the outstanding personal qualities he possessed and which he brought to any game.

Although tall in stature, Eric had a lean frame and did not possess the weight, strength or size to bully and batter his opponents into submission. Rather, he used his rugby brain, allied to his vast array of running and handling skills, to dominate and help his side to victory. As with all great players, his intelligence was at work long before he received the ball. He knew immediately what was to be done as soon as it reached his fingertips. Eric's long legs and stride could take him clear of any sluggish or hesitant defender, while a sudden and often surprising switch of gear could take him past and around an even speedier marker. Ever upright in his stance, he was a stylish player who relished confounding his opposite number (in those days when we had no such abomination as squad numbers) by ability alone. On the representative front, his own haul of 30 tries and 21 tries respectively, against centres of the quality of Australia's Harry Wells and Reg Gasnier whilst on Lions tour duty down under in 1958 and 1962, not to mention the scores he created on that stage for wing partners such as Billy Boston, Ike Southward, Frank Carlton and others, testify further to his international standing.

However, the respect in which Eric was held was never simply down to attacking prowess alone. To be a complete player in a threequarter line, defence must also be a priority. And although, as I indicated earlier, Eric did not have the sort of physique that would allow him to smash opponents into the ground, he did possess the speed and positional sense to force a player out wide to the touchline, where their progress would then be halted by a flawless cover tackle around the legs or hips. Long in the leg, he had arms to match. Like those of an octopus, they seemed to stretch ever longer and never failed to grasp hold of a shirt collar, a flapping jersey or a pair of shorts, if ever a runner looked likely to pass him.

Then again, those long, flailing arms could get him into trouble. While playing for St. Helens in the 1966 Challenge

Cup Final, I tried to duck under one when attempting to make a break down the right-hand touchline: Eric's territory. What appeared to be a dangerous short arm tackle earned Eric a severe warning from Mr. Hunt, the referee, but the smile on my face as I lay looking up at Eric from the Wembley turf, and my immediate defence of him to the official, is an indication that he was one of the fairest and most gentlemanly of players, highly-regarded by all who faced him. All in all, Eric Ashton was a pure footballer and the classy, creative type of centre which, sadly, the rules and style of the modern game do not appear to encourage at the highest levels. Perhaps, today, St. Helens' stylish Australian centre Matt Gidley is one of the few players in the same mould. It is surely no coincidence that Gidley's wing partner, Ade Gardner, ended the 2008 season on top of the cup and league try-scoring lists.

With Eric Ashton alongside him, then, it's little wonder that Billy Boston was such a force to be reckoned with. Billy scored over 50 tries a season three times whilst in Wigan colours, among a host of other fine individual records. That wasn't all down to Eric, of course. Billy was a sensational performer in his own right, who scored an amazing total of 571 tries for Wigan, Blackpool and his representative sides. Of those, 478 were scored for Wigan alone and the majority were at least partly the result of Eric Ashton's rugby genius; he provided the sort of service that any great winger would relish.

Ashton and Boston. What a fine partnership they were and how sides went to any lengths to stop them from causing mayhem down the right wing. I well recall, before one particularly fierce Boxing day derby between St. Helens and Wigan at Knowsley Road, how our loose forward, Billy Major, and I planned to stop the duo from employing their famously devastating crossfield scissors movement. Billy (Major) was instructed to race away quickly from any scrum in midfield, 20 metres from our try-line, and track Eric across the pitch, before tackling him with or without the ball. As for myself, I agreed to move away from the scrum a little more slowly and accepted the daunting task of attempting to stop Boston - all 15 stone of him - as he came thundering in on the inside from Ashton's reverse pass. Again, with or without the ball! Unfortunately, Billy Major broke too slowly from the scrum, while I broke too early. The Wigan pair executed their delightful scissors move as planned, resulting in a try for Boston under the posts, while I mistakenly felled the wrong Billy - our own loose forward - with a perfectly delivered high tackle that resulted in him receiving eight stitches in a cut to the forehead, on the touchline. They really were a fearsome sight in full flight, Eric and Billy. And when, towards the end of his playing career, Eric became the first rugby league player ever to be honoured by the Queen, when he was given an MBE for services to rugby league in 1966, the award was richly deserved.

Although that proud event coincided with the original year of publication of the book you are about to read, Eric's achievements in the 13-a-side code were far from over yet. Even at the height of his playing career with Wigan, he was already turning his thoughts to coaching and, in the early 'sixties, initially fulfilled that role as player-coach. Such a move was to be expected for, in all of the ways already described, Eric possessed every characteristic needed to mould others and withstand the pressures heaped on any coach. And again I firmly believe that those days in the sun, playing touch rugby on a local field, were the ideal training ground.

At just fifteen years of age and already on his way to a height of six-foot plus, Eric towered above many of the youngsters who played alongside him and who literally looked up to him for guidance and authority. He provided it and relished an opportunity to direct play, give instructions and organise the games for both teams. Even as a teenager he commanded an overview and with a snap of his fingers or a short, sharp instruction, proved himself to be a born leader and the ideal captain.

His coaching career, when it duly materialised, lasted until 1980, during which time, after starting as player-coach with Wigan in 1963 and then becoming coach from 1969 to 1973, he also enjoyed a season at Leeds before, in 1974, taking over at St. Helens. And for Eric, even after swapping his boots for a suit, Championship and Challenge Cup wins continued to be par for the course. Ever was he able to illustrate one of the major qualities necessary for anyone who aspires to manage a team. Whether as a captain or coach, Eric could stand back from the action raging around him, detach himself from the immediate problem, survey the damage, and assess what needed to be done. To paraphrase the poet Rudyard Kipling: 'If you can keep your head when all about are losing theirs...' then you are able to lead and to coach. Eric Ashton remained calm amid the most difficult of circumstances, disciplined his troops or players accordingly, and made any decisions with objectivity. When required, he led from the front and all followed.

I particularly admired his coaching skills in two most contrasting of games, especially in terms of their importance to Eric's own coaching career and the sport of rugby league at large. When I had the pleasure of playing for St. Helens against Eric's team, Wigan, in the aforementioned 1966 Challenge Cup final, he was then player-coach to an ageing side which was beaten, 21-2. Although he had difficulty in getting his team to match the Saints' display, he coaxed and cajoled such performances out of many of his players that for a considerable time we were never quite able to claim the victory. Eric's words and his actions raised some players above a level that they were unable to sustain for the full eighty minutes and, though many in the 98,536 crowd were unable to appreciate it, his personality was the thing that kept Wigan as a force until the end.

In 1969, before and during a match played at Central

Park as a part of his well-earned testimonial season, played between St. Helens-born and Wigan-born teams, he displayed as much professionalism as a player-coach to we St. Helens-born players in a knockabout match as he did with Wigan at Wembley. His concentration and application that day was no less than that employed in some of his greatest campaigns. That is why he remains one of the finest coaches that I have ever observed during my sixty years as a spectator, player and commentator.

Eric's amazing career was to take another pathway when, in 1992, with his coaching days behind him, he accepted a position as director with the hometown club that had turned him down as a player all those years before - St. Helens. Again, he filled the role with distinction. Eric served at Knowsley Road for over fifteen years and, as chairman, had the distinction of leading the team out ahead of its Challenge Cup final triumph over Bradford Bulls in 1996, at Wembley. Remarkably, this made Eric Ashton a unique Challenge Cup winner in all three disciplines - captain, coach and chairman. Once again, he proved that he had what it takes to become the driving force behind a club. Having played with and coached many of the sport's greatest players, he introduced that quality of knowledge to Knowsley Road and created the off-field conditions in which such world class talent was able to flourish. Eric's vast experience in the game enabled him to approach any problem with the confidence that he could solve it. He was ever willing to offer shrewd and quiet advice to anyone who needed it, including myself.

Although Eric was unable to play in the second, New Zealand leg of the Lions Tour in 1962, during the earlier matches in Australia, when he captained the Great Britain side, he produced some of the finest rugby of his career. Indeed, whether in that year's Ashes triumph or in the so-called 'lesser' tour matches 'up country', Eric displayed the qualities and temperament that were to mark him out as one of the truly great rugby league players of all time, and one fully deserving of his belated entry into the sport's fabled Hall of Fame in 2005.

In 1962, from Wagga Wagga to Lismore, from Perth to Wollongong, and from Brisbane to Sydney, Eric Ashton revelled in his role of captain and collected 21 tries in just 15 appearances. He further proved - if anyone still doubted it - how creative he could be as a centre, by having a hand in three tries for his wing partner, Billy Boston, in the opening two Tests of the campaign (an even more impressive feat when you consider that in both those games he was confronted by the greatest Kangaroos centre of them all, Reg Gasnier). And while those fifteen games in '62 were but a tiny fraction of those played by Eric throughout his long and varied career - he captained Great Britain to World Cup glory in 1960 too, lest we forget - they surely epitomise all that this gentleman of rugby league was about.

Respected by all who played with or against him, and revered by supporters of those usually intense rivals Wigan and St. Helens alike - a telling situation if ever there was one - Eric bestrode rugby league like a colossus, both on and off the field. Certainly, there are many still serving our great game who are all the better equipped for playing it, coaching it or managing it, after having met him.

In March 2008, after a typically courageous battle with cancer, Eric Ashton MBE passed away, aged 73. It should go without saying that Eric's death was met with great sadness by everyone who loved, knew or admired him. One thing, however, is for sure. The memory of a true gentleman and his outstanding impact on the game of rugby league football will shine on - gloriously - forever.

Glory in the centre spot, indeed.

Introduction

Glory In The Centre Spot

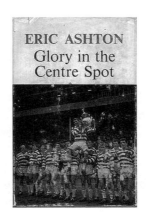

ERIC ASHTON
Glory in the
Centre Spot

Original foreword (1966)
By Jack Nott
News of the World rugby league writer

There are many Rugby League fans who have never met Eric Ashton, of Wigan and international fame. To them, he is just a name on a team-sheet or in the sports columns of a newspaper.

A pity. For Ashton is the epitome of the hero. The Western hero. He is the lean, tall, taciturn character who would ride with John Wayne.

And, like Wayne, he always fights fair.

In a game which has been libelled and slandered for so-called rough-stuff, Eric has never applied violence.

It is not his nature to do so.

He has levered his way to the very top by way of the skillful hand-off.

He is Mr Wigan. And, because of the standing that Central Park holds in the Rugby League game, this makes him Mr Rugby League.

You know his history as well as I do.

Ashton was born in St Helens. The Saints could have scooped him up. But don't knock Knowsley Road. They have made few mistakes. This just happened to be one of them.

And this sort of thing has happened in many spheres. I know a British actor who had to go as far as Hollywood in order to get recognition.

Eric Ashton found fame nearer to home.... at Wigan.

There he became club captain, then player-manager-coach. He was made Great Britain's skipper. He made twenty-six appearances for his country - in the days when Great Britain's Rugby League Lions were a mighty force.

Now, although he has retired from international duties, I would like it to be very much on the cards that Ashton goes to Australia this summer as our touring side's tactician-in-chief.

But Ashton is more than a series of statistics. He is a family man whom I like to call a friend.

I have had many an after-the-game chat with him. When he is on a win bonus he will dissect the game - but rarely with any mention of his own all-powerful contribution.

If he is on losing pay he will put forward the same clinical analysis. Only this time he will feature himself among the team's shortcomings.

Which, nine times out of ten, is nonsense. For rarely does Ashton play an incompetent game.

The top brass of Rugby League have dreamt up all sorts of ideas to keep the keel even in the professional rugby code. Two divisions and new legislation have been just two of them. A waste of time.

What is wanted: More Ernest Wards, more Ken Traills .... and certainly more Eric Ashtons.

Ashton, likable, authoritative, and the perfect club or country captain, has found more than glory in the centre spot.

He has earned his title - Mr. Rugby League - the hard way. With drive ... drive ... drive. He had the ability. Brilliance naturally followed.

As I have said, we could do with more like Eric Ashton in this grand game of Rugby League.

Author's Note

I would like to thank Arthur Brooks and Malcolm Keogh for their assistance while this book was being compiled.

E.A.

Glory In The Centre Spot

1

A NUMBER 352 BUS TO FAME

I was standing in a spot which feels slightly higher than Mount Everest, and a heck of a lot noisier. All around me, ninety-thousand screaming and shouting fanatics were making it that way.

The spot - right outside the Royal box at Wembley Stadium. And, in my business, that is about as high as you can go and still keep your hat on.

I had just been handed the most glittering prize of the lot - the Rugby League Challenge Cup. And right at that moment I loved everyone in that howling crowd, except that they were making so much din I couldn't hear what the American ambassador was talking about.

Not that it mattered much. All that did matter was that I was there. Right on top of the world. And in two days I would be heading for the other side of it, to start my second Australian tour.

Just three short years after it all began ...

With the kind of mistake only a kid can make. A kid with too many stars in his eyes and not enough money in his pocket to reach them. Mistake? Well, even looking back on it, over the bruising and bone-cracking glory, it still looks that way to me. And why?

It kicked me off on the kind of life that has shot me into a million back-slaps and cheers. It gave me the biggest job I can hope for - captain of Great Britain. And it nearly gave my dad apoplexy ...

The mistake? I made it on the day I leaned over a table and scratched my name on the bottom of a piece of paper. The day I signed on to become a professional player for the biggest Rugby League glory-spinners of them all, Wigan.

Maybe I had better go back to where it all started. A long time before the screaming crowds, the gleaming trophies, the sweat and the big money.

Right back to a little pub singer, the guard-room on an army camp in Scotland, and a bus ride I took with exactly one pound in my wallet.

Bus rides - the ones on the Number 352 from my home on a council estate in St Helens to the Wigan ground at Central Park - have had some odd endings for me.

There was the time I got off ... and walked straight into the news that they had picked me for my first Australian tour.

This one wasn't quite like that, back in July, 1955, when I got my first look into the inside of big-time Rugby League. Australia was just one big dot on the map. And the nearest I had been to it was looking at the dot.

That was in the geography lessons at the Rivington School in St Helens. I got my first taste of what was coming there, when they picked me for the town schoolboys' team.

Where I lived, down Mulberry Avenue, you could spit on a windy day and nearly reach the ground where the local big shots, the Saints, would pack in the crowds every other Saturday. Rugby was tea and supper down Mulberry Avenue, usually with a tin can for a ball and the knees torn out of your pants when it was all over.

Those games with the town schoolboys were the high-spots. And the Saturdays when the Saints were at home to all-comers were even higher. You needed money to see that - or, anyway, you should have done. We didn't most times. There was another way. Straight over a wall, through the men's toilets and into the crowd. It worked a treat, and I reckon the days when I was their biggest fan cost St Helens a packet.

Anyway, for me, it was worth it. That way I got my first look at the two men I would try to copy when the tin can came out again afterwards.

One was Jimmy Stott, the Saints' centre and captain. A tubby, homely-looking bloke, but a marvellous player. It was a funny thing about the other one. He didn't even play for the Saints. In fact, he was the star for their arch enemies - Wigan. Ernie Ashcroft.

It's even funnier when you think how it was going to work out. But that comes later.

Like the rest, I wanted to move out of the boys' pen and play. It was the kind of thing we all dreamed about in the pen.

For me it came true ... or, at least, I got the chance to make it come true. That was when I got the heftiest slap in the face I've ever had ... and officially retired from Rugby League at the ripe old age of 16. After all, getting the frozen shoulder from someone you worship is always hard. Especially when you reckon that before long they are going to start worshipping you. That is what happened when I rolled up for my first trial with the Saints' 'B' team, after signing up on amateur forms.

I had a good game - or so I thought. And afterwards I waited for the next one to show I could be even better. The only trouble was, nobody seemed interested in finding out.

The offer didn't come. Not even the offer of another try out with the 'B' team. Just silence.

The weekly training sessions began to be a bit of a bore,

with nothing at the end but more training. I was mad at Saints. They weren't even interested enough to be mad at me.

So I quit. Officially. Eric Ashton, future international, future globe-trotter, became Eric Ashton, ex-promising Rugby League player.

For two years I didn't want to know about Rugby League. Life was a job at the local glassworks and a night out with the boys.

It took the British Army to bring me out of retirement. The Army and the nasty habit they have of making you do guard duties on wet nights. I was sent up to Edinburgh to start my National Service as a Royal Artillery gunner. And gunners do guard duties.

But there is one thing you find out right away in the army. If you can kick a ball, or throw one, or smack somebody on the chin with a boxing glove, the guard duties don't come around so often.

So when they asked for volunteers for the regimental Rugby Union team, who should be right in line for a place but Gunner Ashton, the former Rugby League player of no repute.

And if the Saints didn't like the way I played, the army thought it was all right. They kept me in the team, even picked me for Scottish Command, and gave me trials for the Army side in London. That is a lot of guard duties!

What really mattered about those games with the Army was the introduction they gave me to Bert Marsh, the regimental scrum-half. He was a pretty good scrum-half, too, with another sideline in singing in the pubs and clubs.

Bert came from Wigan, and he was pretty pally with some of the boys from Central Park. I still don't know whether they had asked him to be a sort of unofficial talent spotter in the army. But whatever it was he kept plugging Wigan - and asking me to have a go with them when I got out. Which was how I came to be sitting in the bar of the

Royal Oak, in Wigan, sipping a pint and talking to one of
their directors, Billy Woods.

'Give it a try, lad', he said. 'Just go along and play. You've
got nothing to lose.'

At least somebody was asking me to play. It was a
change from just hanging around and training ... then
training again.

Two days later I hopped on the 352 and headed for Central
Park. And it worked. They offered me six trials straight off.

They were six games I never played in. Because at Wigan
I got a slice of luck tossed right into my lap without even
asking for it. I arrived at Central Park to watch the public
trial before the season started - and was told: 'Get changed.
You are playing.'

Just like that. Without even seeing what I could do they
were throwing me in against their hard-bitten first-teamers.
I didn't know whether it was a dream or a nightmare.

I knew as soon as I stepped out on the pitch, though. It
was going to be more like a horror film with five 'X'
certificates. For standing there, waiting to mark me, and a bit
browned off with the chore, was my old idol Ernie Ashcroft.

That game is still a bit muddled up in my mind. All I
know is that, as far as I was concerned, it worked. I got two
tries and kicked some goals as well. Old Ernie didn't put
anything over on me at all.

I felt pretty cocky about that. But, I have to admit, it was
the end of the summer lay-off. Ernie must have been a bit
soft and out of condition, like the rest of the stars. It is
probably as well for me that he was.

In the dressing-room after it was all over, somebody
shouted through the steam: 'Ashton, you are wanted in the
boardroom.'

And I remember Ernie saying: 'Make them pay for it,
boy.' Maybe I should have taken more notice of what he said.
That was the mistake I told you about - the one that still
makes me wince every time I think about it.

In the boardroom the directors were waiting. Shrewd-looking, well-dressed and experienced. 'We want you to sign for us,' one of them said. 'There is £150 in it for you.'

Right then I had one pound in my pocket. With that kind of money behind you, £150 sounds like the crock of gold. I signed ... and I've never stopped kicking myself since.

I don't blame Wigan too much for it. They wanted to sign somebody they fancied - and they didn't want to throw too much money around to get him. After all, I was just a kid and they had seen me play only one game.

Yet I am convinced I could have got more - a lot more - if I had made them wait. I believe they would have paid.

After all, these days they are snapping up the rawest Rugby Union players without any idea about what they can do in the rougher, tougher League game. And they never even start talking business under £500.

As far as money goes, I've made more than enough since to cover that bit lost. But it still rankles that I didn't hold out for more.

My father thought so, too. He is Ernie Ashton, the ex-Warrington centre. And he knows the game backwards - on the field and off. When he found out what I'd done he was almost angry enough to make me an ex-Wigan player before I had even started.

You see, I was twenty the day I signed. I should have had his permission. But I was walking on so much air at being asked that I kidded Wigan about my age. I told them I was twenty-one.

My dad nearly lifted the roof off the little house in Mulberry Avenue when I walked in waving my cheque, and told him what I had done. He threatened to rip up the forms - and I have never talked more than I did that night to make him change his mind.

I think we are both glad he did. Like I said, that £150 doesn't seem like much now, and he has turned into one of Wigan's biggest fans since. But Wigan never knew how close they came to a boardroom blow-up ... and losing the services of their latest signing in record time.

A lesson, a cheque and a contract weren't the only things I took out of that public trial at Wigan. I collected my first scars as well. The skin was ripped from both my knees, and it was two weeks before I got chance to line up and find out what it was really all about.

It turned out to be quite a season, that first one at Wigan playing in front of the most critical crowd in the game. For that is what the Wigan fans are. They know the game as well as you do, every move of it. They are used to big things. And if they don't get them there is hell to play.

If any one of the thirteen of us was off-form in a match they could break our hearts. If we clicked, they could make us feel like kings.

But it wasn't long - seven weeks to be precise - before I got a taste of what it can be like playing outside the white-hot fury of the league circus and the partisan crowds.

I was picked for my first representative game, and after just seven matches. It was pretty rapid, to say the least. And at that time it was the worst thing that could have happened to me.

The game? Lancashire against New Zealand at Warrington. It was one honour I still think I could have done without. I played a stinker. A real stinker.

The crowds at games like that don't get so worked-up. For them, there isn't all that much at stake. It was just as well for me. They let me off lightly. If they had given me the bird I couldn't have blamed them.

Lancashire picked me on the wing. I couldn't do a thing right. Top-class Rugby League was still pretty new to me. And the pace in this one was just too much. When it was over I remember thinking to myself: 'If that is being honoured, they can keep it.' I've changed my mind since. But then I meant every word of it.

It was about the only black spot in that first season. The

rest of it went like a celluloid success story. I wound up with 28 tries under my belt.

The only black spot, did I say? Well, almost. There was another that was more of a running streak than a spot. It went right through the season.

And that was the position that Wigan insisted I should play in. On the wing. I didn't like it. Oh, I know, I was scoring the tries - and that is what really counts when they pay out your wages. But I never was a winger. Never. My position had always been in the centre. That is where I am happiest. On the wing I usually felt lost - out of it - just hanging around for the breaks to come my way instead of making them.

I pleaded with Wigan to put me in the centre. They wouldn't listen. Every time the team list came out there was Ashton - back on the wing.

I even threatened them, told them I wouldn't play and asked to go into the 'A' team. All this from the bloke who hadn't yet been there twelve months, and who had been rejected, anyway, by his home-town team!

Wigan reckoned they knew best. Right until the time, at the start of the next season, the man I admire more than anyone else in this business came along.

His name ... Joe Egan. Wigan made him their coach. He had already gone down among the immortals as one of their greatest-ever players. Now they wanted him to get Wigan back to the greatness from which they had slipped.

Well, Joe Egan did it. And the job didn't break a single heart. He was - and still is - a gentleman. The kind who can get the best out of you without lifting his voice above a whisper.

Gentleman Joe did that for me. He started off by giving me the centre spot I had been asking for. Since then I have done pretty well all there is to do in our Rugby League game. I am convinced that the one reason I have been able to do it is Joe Egan.

He gave Wigan what they wanted - a new brand of glory. When it ended the way it did no one was sadder than I was. It is old history that Wigan fired Joe just after St Helens licked us at Wembley 1961 in the Rugby League Challenge Cup Final.

Why they did it is, I suppose, Wigan's business. And Joe Egan's. He still came out on top, doing a great job of whipping Widnes into shape once he took over their reins.

That was Widnes' good luck. While he was with them that was Wigan's good luck. It was the biggest disappointment of my career that it had to end.

But that is Rugby League. And when Joe, the gentle genius, came along it was the signal for me to really start learning what it was all about.

Glory In The Centre Spot

2

THE GENTLE GENIUS

For a long, glorious run with Wigan Joe Egan walked really tall with his pocket Hercules 5ft. 8in. frame.

Hooker supreme and the pride of Wigan. A bloke who cut his words to the absolute minimum in any conversation - but made every syllable count. The toughest and craftiest player ever to don a Number Nine jersey in Rugby League football. The slightly bandy-legged hero of more than TEN THOUSAND scrums.

That was the pride of Wigan, where the world's most ardent Rugby League fans used to call him 'Joe Ay-gan', as they supped their pints in their clubs and pubs.

Lancashire folk - and especially Wiganers - aren't daft. They pay their best on a Saturday afternoon to see the best. Nowt but the best. And in Joe, whether they pronounced his surname Ay-gan or Ee-gan, they got just that.

Joe, former Wigan and England Test captain, delighted his beloved town of Wigan all his career except for those six years as player-coach at Leigh, from 1950-56.

Egan, as a hooker, was the Joe Louis of his time. I owe

much to this Gentle Genius. But, before talking about Egan the coach, let me dip into the record of Egan the player.

It was in November, 1950, that the glorious career of this outstanding forward ended at Headingley, Leeds.

Joe - Cap'n Joe - was retiring from Test R.L. football when he had played his thirty-third and last representative game for his country.

Since he had been first chosen for a representative honour in 1942, Egan, a master of Rugby tactics and a hooker of the highest possible ability, had never been dropped.

When he trotted out on his cowboy legs at Headingley on November 11, 1950, he had already played in 14 Tests (five against New Zealand), ten times for England against Wales, seven matches against France, and once against Other Nationalities.

Naturally, therefore, Joe's passing from the international scene was not only regretted by followers of the professional code in his own country, but by the many enthusiasts overseas - Australia, New Zealand and France - who had been delighted by his remarkable play.

As a forward when at his peak, Egan was simply matchless. His skill, both in scrummaging and in the loose, contributed largely to Wigan's all-round supremacy in Rugby League football.

As their captain he led them magnificently. Shortly before that final good-bye to international football, however, Egan had been transferred to Leigh as their player-coach, and for a then record fee for a forward of £5,000.

It was for that reason that Egan, who has been described as 'the best and fairest hooker of all time', felt compelled to relinquish his international duties, and pass on his experience, wisdom and skill to his new young forward colleagues at neighbouring Leigh.

Egan had moved to our Central Park club at Wigan in 1937, following his Rugby apprenticeship with four local teams: St Patrick's Schoolboys, St Patrick's Old Boys, Wigan Highfield Old Boys and St Patrick's Juniors.

Egan went on and on, once he had won outstanding recognition, simply collecting fame in Northern Rugby League, at Wembley Stadium, and in Australia, New Zealand and France.

He became a leader of the finest calibre; a forward who could sense a break-through immediately, and exploit it with a sudden switch of strategy that quickly stamped him as an artist. His passes were made to look so easy, yet they proved so effective.

In the scrums he invariably commanded a mastery over his opponent by an amazing ability and intelligence which came only from the blend of genius and experience.

No finer tribute could have been paid Egan, on the eve of his last game for England, than the one by Mr. W.H.Hughes, chairman of the Rugby League Selection Committee, who said: 'The success of the teams in which you have played - national, county and Wigan - is due in no small measure to the part *you* have played.'

That was Joe Egan the player ... the maestro of hookers whose proudest moment came when he was the only Rugby League captain ever to receive the Challenge Cup trophy at Wembley from the late King George VI ... the hooker who, at his pomp, must have been a priceless prince to Wigan.

Egan faced a new challenge when he switched over to the coaching side of the business at Leigh. One of the biggest challenges - and it's by no means Joe's fault - resulted in a dismal failure.

Rugby League, and especially Leigh, won't exactly thank me for mentioning the name McDonald Bailey, the ace Jamaican sprinter who jumped on to the R.L. bandwagon when tempted with a big-money offer.

Now 'Mac' Bailey had been a sensational success at the Olympics. Leigh directors thought he was going to be just as red-hot on the playing pitch as he was on the running track.

And the unenviable job of trying to make a Rugby League winger out of 'Mac' was given to poor Joe!

An impossible task right from the start. We all know Berwyn Jones has certainly made the grade with Wakefield Trinity. But in 1953, at Leigh, McDonald Bailey never 'broke any pots' with his new team-mates or Rugby League supporters alike.

Egan devised a rota system of players to attend the ground for training with 'The Brown Flash', in order to show him the art of the sidestep, the tackle, and the way to take hard knocks.

It meant a lot of hard work for Mr J.E. and for Mr McB., who soon knew what he was up against, and speedily worked out a new chart of exercises for himself.

The late Mr Jim Hilton, Leigh's popular chairman at the time, said: 'McDonald Bailey is an intelligent man. He knows what he is up against and is determined to make good at it.'

But determination wasn't enough. Even the coaching, coaxing and cajoling of Joe Egan wasn't enough, either. A miracle was needed. And miracles never happen in Rugby League.

McDonald Bailey, his bank balance admittedly looking more healthy, bowed himself out of our game almost as soon as he had got his boots dirty.

In August, 1956, Joe Egan became the new boss at Wigan, indeed a happy return for the local lad who had learned his football as a schoolboy in Wigan, became the idol of Central Park's fans, and the greatest hooker-forward the game has known.

Leigh chairman, Hilton, announced that Egan's five-year contract, which had started in 1953, had terminated in complete agreement and full harmony with the club. He added, 'We are sorry to lose Joe, but we would not stand in his way. We wish him well at Central Park.'

Joe's happiness at Central Park, like his five years' contract, lasted ... JUST FIVE YEARS.

Wigan sacked their ace coach twenty days after our team's shock defeat by St Helens in the Rugby League Cup Final at Wembley.

Forty-one-year-old Egan, who had taken us to Wembley three times and guided us to a league championship in five seasons, had quizzed Wigan about his future. Their reply: 'We don't intend to renew your contract.'

At the time, as the Wigan captain, I thought it was unjust pinning the blame for that Wembley defeat on Joe - and possibly making that the main reason for firing him from his Central Park job.

Whether Egan was going to be sacked if we won or not against Saints, the 'old enemy', I'm afraid I can't answer.

I do know that it was something more than a Cup Final in May, 1961. We were playing St Helens - and they have always been, particularly to our directors and supporters, our deadliest enemies.

Also, I do know there had been some rumours flying around Wigan and other Rugby League circles, concerning Joe's future with us at Central Park.

It still came as a bombshell when I returned from holiday to discover that he had not been re-engaged as our coach.

But B always follows A in a boardroom. Only results count with club directors or committeemen. Only a minority of them can accept defeat like a player.

Certainly, something concerning Egan had gone wrong behind the scenes.

And now, I feel, is the right time to give my view on two important aspects of the Egan affair ...

It was through no fault of Joe's coaching that we lost to Saints at Wembley. We were the favourites. We had the ability. And we did our best.

Three times under his guidance I captained Wigan at Wembley. In 1958, the year after Joe had taken over the Wigan reins, we beat Workington Town by 13 points to nine (attendance 66,000; receipts £31,030). The following year we defeated Hull by 30 points to 13 (attendance 80,000; receipts £33,000).

Furthermore, at the end of the 1959-60 season we whipped Wakefield Trinity by 27 points to 3 in the Rugby League Championship Final at Bradford's Odsal Stadium. And, only a few days' previously, Trinity had walloped Hull 38-5 in the Wembley Challenge Cup Final.

Not a bad record for Joe Egan, was it? By the way, in those '58 and '59 Wembley-winning finals we had Rees Thomas and Brian McTigue winning the Lance Todd Trophy for the best individual performances.

But, I almost forgot, there was that little matter of our defeat by St Helens which, the more you think about it, must have been a contributing factor to Egan's departure from Central Park.

Now Wigan are always favourites in *any* match or *any* final. This time, with Saints' Ken Large breaking our back and Karalius and Huddart our spirit, we didn't come out on top.

Still, Egan's record was still outstanding: Two wins out of three trips to Wembley in five seasons, plus that championship title.

As you may have guessed, it's hard to read some directors' minds at times!

In club or international football I have served under quite a number of coaches: Egan, Ted Ward, Jim Sullivan, Alan Prescott, Griff Jenkins, Colin Hutton, Jim Brough and Rugby League Secretary Bill Fallowfield.

Egan was the best. I have picked up something useful from each of them. Unfortunately, I hadn't the opportunity to work with 'Sully' for long. Simply because Jim Sullivan, one of the finest coaches our game has ever had, was already in failing health when he rejoined us after spells at St Helens and Rochdale Hornets. And he only stayed for about three months before illness took a firmer grip on this perfectionist, hard taskmaster, and firm friend of any player, either youthful or veteran, whose heart was in the right place.

So, give me Egan every time. He was tactful and rarely lost his temper. He was never bombastic and rarely railroaded a player. He commanded respect and, while using mainly orthodox coaching methods, had infinite patience with youngsters.

One Wigan fan once summed-up one of our wins over a Yorkshire team with typical Lancashire bluntness: 'Yon lot has been EGANISED'.

Well, within seventeen days of leaving us as coach, Joe Egan was signing another contract ... as manager-coach at Widnes on a three-year contract.

In May, 1964, Joe Egan was on familiar ground again .. at Wembley. And what did his Widnes boys to do Hull Kingston Rovers? Well, pardon me, but they Eganised 'em!

Glory In The Centre Spot

3

FIVE TRIPS TO WEMBLEY

May Day! It's the world-wide yell for help when you suddenly find you are right up against it; when you get an overpowering wish to reach out and clutch at something safe and reassuring; when you are swamped by an unshakeable fear that you are going to be sunk without trace.

Well, I have never been a sailor in distress. I have never had to ditch a plane, either. But I have known five May Days, all right. Or, to be exact, five days in May when every one of those uneasy feelings has jolted clean through me. Five days when I have stepped out of a dark tunnel. And on to the great, flat, green torture rack called Wembley.

Torture is the word. Because nothing - and I mean nothing - can match those final few minutes before the start of a Cup Final, for testing the stretching power of your nerves. And that goes double when you know you are the man who, at the end of it, will either be lifting that fancy silver pot, or just leading twelve other probably angry and certainly despondent men to collect the losers' medals that tell them they were only second best.

All of this will tell you why those five bright Saturdays when I have been Wigan's cup final captain, have left me with some of my best - and some of my most agonising - memories.

And it will also tell you why Saturday, May 8, 1965, stands out as the day I most want to remember when the rest of the glory days and the gory days have started to fade.

It was the day I didn't just lead Wigan up for the cup. It was the day I knew I had made it in the other big role I had taken on. The role of coaching, cajoling and finally picking the team that beat the huskies from Hunslet in the final they are now calling the greatest of them all.

I can tell you ... there will never be a day like that. It was the one day I have felt fully entitled to feel just a little big-headed. Yes, that hard-earned beating of Hunslet was the biggest paving-stone on my Wembley road. But while I was being handed that cup, getting my hair mussed up and my back slapped until it was sore, my mind kept going back to the first of the five.

Remember it? May 10, 1958, when suddenly, so far as Rugby League went, I felt I had grown up. Because you have to grow up pretty fast when you are thrust into the Wembley furnace at the head of a hard-bitten, success-hungry outfit like Wigan. And when you know it is not going to be any walk-over.

Workington have never been a walk-over. This wasn't going to be any exception. Just take a look at the line-up we had to face. It included half-backs like Sol Roper and Harry Archer, clever and experienced: A well-knitted partnership. It included winger Ike Southward, one of the deadliest try-scoring machines in the game. And it included that second-row maestro Brian Edgar, on his day pretty well unstoppable.

Sitting in the dressing-room, and feeling the nerves bunching up, it was Edgar who was on my mind most of all. Give him any room at all, I kept saying to myself, and we have had it. And I am going to look a right twerp.

For, really, behind all the tension, the weak jokes and the celebrations, the Cup Final is still a game of Rugby. And that means you have to pluck out the enemy's biggest sting - and kill it off.

We had talked about Edgar long and hard at Central Park while we drilled ourselves into readiness for the big test. He is one of my best friends, but I think I managed to convince myself he was my biggest enemy. Edgar had to go!

While I sat and worried about Workington's big, bustling spearhead, I had one ray of hope in the back of my mind. They had Edgar. But we had Brian McTigue. And it was to McTigue that I said: 'You have to see him off. That's your job.'

Mac just nodded and, like the great pro. he is, stepped out and did precisely that. He got to Edgar early on, and really blasted him hard. By the time McTigue had finished working him over, Edgar wasn't much of a force in that particular game. He was shaken up. And he wilted, while Mighty McTigue rampaged on and finally got the try that really sealed it for us.

It was a peach. With the whole Workington defence hanging back and expecting him to shoot an outside pass, Brian, the crafty old fox, hung on to the ball and dummied his way clear through the lot of them to burst over in the corner.

But if McTigue, the watchdog and the try scorer, cut himself an outsize slice of glory that day, a man a lot smaller carved himself an even bigger one. The name: Rees Thomas, the supreme club servant.

Rees was never a glory hunter. Just a guy who had been around for a long time, knew what it was all about, took the knocks and never moaned about them.

No, Rees never looked for the applause. But I was never so glad that he had answered Wigan's own May Day call, as I was when I watched him go to work on Workington. He did everything, poured his whole heart into it, brought out every scrap of his enormous skill. And he left Workington reeling dizzily.

What's more, Rees, imported to help stitch Wigan together so that we could recapture the old success days, finally got the recognition he deserved. They voted him the Lance Todd Trophy winner when he had finished with Workington.

Rees Thomas' personal success story is all the more fitting, when you remember he hadn't even been one hundred per cent sure of getting a place in the Final team. That season we had been experimenting with a new half back combination of Dave Bolton and Billy Boston.

But it was Rees who had pulled out all the stops, when he was given the chance, to get us to Wembley. He had scorched Oldham in our toughest match, that third round clash on our Wembley trail.

Rees never again hit the heights that he reached against Workington. He had accomplished the task for which Wigan wanted him. He had provided the sheer, old-headed skill we so vitally needed while we got set to become the game's biggest force once again. And he earned the undying gratitude of every Wigan fan who had feared that the days of Ryan, Mountford, Gee and Egan would never come to Central Park again.

I will always remember him for that ...

But I won't remember all that much about my own personal role in that 13-9 defeat of Workington. It simply wasn't one of the best games I have had. I don't think I did too much that was wrong. But any glory that was going went to McTigue. To Mick Sullivan, who stamped his class all over his try, which followed a movement right across the back division. And, above all, to little Rees Thomas.

The one thing you never expect to get as you work, eat and sleep through those tension-packed weeks before Wembley is an easy ride when you finally get there.

After all, why should you? You know exactly what is

waiting for you. Thirteen other tough, keen and keyed-up men whose biggest aim in life is to knock your head off.

That is why, in a way, May 9, in the year after I suddenly grew up against the precision power of Workington, ranks as one of the most DISAPPOINTING I have faced.

Disappointing? Yes, because after all that doubting, wondering and planning, it rocks you right back on your heels to find that the men you have been dreaming about and half-fearing, just bow down humbly and allow themselves to be slaughtered.

In a way, it knocks a lot of the gilt off the biggest day of the year. Bowing down - and getting slaughtered - is exactly what Hull, the rugged pride of Yorkshire, did when we came face to face with them in front of 80,000 witnesses, and smashed them to a 30 points to 13 defeat.

It was so easy. And it left us holding two records. We became the first team to win the Cup two years in succession. And we walked off with Wembley's biggest-ever points tally.

The second, quite honestly, I could have done without. As I have said, you get a much bigger kick when you know it has been tough and you have STILL won.

I don't know what went wrong with Hull. There certainly wasn't any doubt that they weren't a pushover outfit. Before May 9, anyway. Their coach, Roy Francis, reckoned they didn't follow his orders. I can believe that!

Francis also said afterwards that our move in switching our props, John Barton and Bill Bretherton, was a master stroke in helping us to win possession from the scrums.

Maybe the plain fact was that their nerves gave way. Whatever is was, we ended up ripping through their cover as easily as though we were enjoying a Tuesday night training session. And that just doesn't happen at Wembley. Or it shouldn't!

We were 20-4 up by half-time, and I have never heard more gay chat than there was from our lads in the dressing-room.

What we had been most scared of was Hull's powerful pack ... and Johnny Whiteley in particular. But they never got going at all, Whiteley included.

When Hull did click - and they certainly launched some promising moves, with only full-back Keegan left in their own half - our defence was superb.

Dave Bolton and McTigue, who got the Lance Todd Trophy this time after missing it the year before, had a field day.

What it really boiled down to in the end was that Hull simply stepped out at Wembley under-equipped. They had the power in the forwards, but nothing in the backs to exploit it.

Maybe I am being a little hard on them when I say they bowed down. The simple truth was that we beat them down with sheer speed. It was almost sad to see Whiteley and the rest trying to get things moving - then standing stunned and staggered every time we whipped into a counter-attack that pushed up the score a little more almost every time.

Can you blame me, or the rest of my boys for that matter, if we drove away from Wembley that day thinking we were, without doubt, the world's greatest. We had ripped Hull apart and left them dumped in a heap.

We had done it in a game about which Peter Wilson, of the *Daily Mirror*, had said: 'I have only one prejudice against Rugby League. Why isn't it played constantly in the south? What a magnificent game the R.L. Cup Final at Wembley was - the best afternoon I've spent in the famous stadium for months, if not years.'

He summed it up further: 'Wigan's split-second opportunism, speed of thought, matched by that of foot, meant that every Hull mistake cost them three points.'

Oh, yes, we were right on top of the world. Right back where Wigan belonged. And I was the man who had led them back to the pinnacle.

It was to be two full years before I came back to Wembley again ... to have the Biggest Day of the Year twanging my nerves again ... to prove that Wigan were still on top of the world.

This time it wasn't going to be against a full-of-holes, slow-moving outfit like Hull. There was no point in anybody at Central Park having the slightest hope that Wigan was going to run up anything approaching a record score.

No chance at all. Because this was the Big One that the whole Rugby League had been waiting for ever to watch. Wigan lining up at Wembley against the team we most love to hate. The old and bitter enemy, St Helens.

This was the one we just had to win, because defeat by St Helens was the one thing that would stick longest in our throats.

This was the one in which it was no use at all detailing off an 'assassin' to take care of the biggest menace on the other side. Because Saints packed so much menace! Menace like Vince Karalius, the 'Wild Bull' who had fully earned that title. Like Dick Huddart, fast, destructive and clever. Like Alex Murphy, who you can't make plans for anyway. And like Tom Van Vollenhoven, the Springbok winger who weaves his own brand of magic.

There was all of this to be faced up to ... and to be beaten. We believed we could do it. They had the speed. We, and there were no doubts on this score, had the sheer football skill and the experience. We were convinced that this was the most valuable commodity to have on your side at Wembley. And we were equally convinced that it would pull us through to the greatest cup victory of all time.

We thought Saints would play it straightforward, relying heavily on their speed. We had our order: 'Take the man and the ball'.

The order went wrong just once. And that was enough to give Wembley one of the most spectacular tries it has ever seen ... and enough to give Wigan the most galling defeat we have ever tasted.

The single moment of tragic truth came in the second half. The irony of it was heightened by the fact that one of the most efficient men I have ever played with was responsible for it. The unfortunate man - the player I could cheerfully have strangled on that brilliant May day, in front of 95,000 fans? None other than Fred 'Punchy' Griffiths, top-class goalkicker and one of the game's really solid full-backs.

Griffiths boobed when he forced the flying Van Vollenhoven into parting with the ball to his centre Ken Large ... but never got round to tackling him. Instead, Van ran out of play - and straight back in again to collect the return from Large and finish off a great move.

I remember watching it all happen as though it were in slow motion. I remember thinking: 'This is it, now. They have beaten us.' And I also remember saying to myself: 'Fred, why the hell did you do that?'

I ran back fully determined to give Griffiths the roasting of his life. But he beat me to it. He just threw up his hands and admitted his mistake. There was nothing that could be done about it.

That try, coming when the Saints were just slightly ahead, sapped the heart out of us. And there is nothing quite like having to face up to that when you are two-thirds of the way through a Cup Final.

You know it is all over, that every effort you have made has been wasted. In short, that you have lost.

That final, too, has gone down as one of the best Wembley has seen. But for me, while I admit that it was packed with excitement and tension, it has left some pretty sour memories.

Not, I want to add, the fact that we lost to St Helens. That, of course, was a hard thing to take, but there is no denying the fact that Saints earned it. If any man had to collect that cup instead of me, I am glad it was Vince Karalius.

The bitterness came AFTERWARDS. The first pill we had to swallow was being paid only £7 a man for the back-breaking effort we had poured into the game, win or lose.

I know we had been told that would be the losing fee. But it seemed precious little to bring home from Wembley.

Especially when you consider that this titanic game pulled record receipts of £35,000!

The second - and, for me, it was an even bigger one to take - was that this was the last game in which we had Joe Egan as our coach. Joe's contract wasn't renewed after we had been licked by Saints. True, that left me with the chance of becoming a coach myself. But it was a sad sight to see Joe leaving the club he had served for so long, under a cloud of rumours that he had been axed because he hadn't pulled off a win against St Helens.

This is a tough game, in which results count. You have to accept that. But my view is that there was nothing at all wrong with the tactics we used against St Helens. We played it the right way. One slip-up beat us. One slip that came two-thirds of the way through the game, when we were still in with a great chance.

The penalties of just one failure can be pretty devastating!

On only one other occasion have I felt the blinding hopelessness that hit me when I saw Vollenhoven racing away, and the cup disappearing into St Helens boardroom.

Naturally, it was reserved for Wembley. For there is nothing than can touch Wembley, on Cup Final day, for reducing even the most hardened professional to feeling extreme emotion.

It was my fourth trip there, this time to face Wakefield Trinity, on yet another of those May days, in 1963.

The easiest thing in the world is to say when it is all over: 'We should have won it'. But I don't make any apology this time for saying it. This was the Final that Wigan zipped into, grasped firmly - and then tossed away.

The record books show that we wound up on the short end of a 25-10 score. Even now it baffles and angers me to think about it. To think about how it could possibly happen after we had rocked Wakefield in a dazzling opening twenty-minutes spell.

Perhaps this will tell you how shaken Trinity were at that stage before the big switch came - and I was again forced to take home a beaten Wigan side.

It happened while Wakefield were reeling. I was standing close to Derek Turner, Wakefield's loose forward, and as hard-bitten a customer as you are ever likely to find.

But so bemused was Turner that he turned to his colleagues in disgust and snapped: 'Come on, for God's sake! Let's at least give them a game'. He was convinced we were going to run up a cricket score. And there wasn't anybody on the ground at that moment who would have argued with him!

But those first golden twenty minutes turned out to be sheer waste, and the turning-point came two minutes before half-time. It was a double hammer blow, and it left Dave Bolton with the saddest Wembley memory. He was knocked cold trying to link up with Geoff Lyon, for a try.

Dave never quite pulled himself together after that. It just wasn't Bolton's day. With the score at 12-7 he slung out a pass that Harold Poynton nipped in to intercept and go over for a try. Neil Fox clipped over the goal and that clinched it for Wakefield.

This was also the Wembley final that turned into a series of agonising 'ifs' for me. I touched down myself in those high-speed opening minutes, after being tackled at the line, but the try was disallowed. A tough one to take.

Another 'if' came when our other centre, Alan Davies, sliced Wakefield wide open with a great run. But Alan tried to make the extra yard, with Frank Carlton in full flight and pleading for the ball. And another chance gone.

Almost the same thing happened after a sizzling burst from Stan McLeod. Stan kept on going, and Wakefield were rattled. But Billy Boston was too far behind. Stan hung on - and down he went under a tackle, when he had only one man left to beat.

All these added up to the most frustrating spell of Rugby League I have ever lived through. Of course, there was no point in expecting Trinity to just hang around waiting to be hit. They pulled themselves together, and when they started swinging we were on the run.

The truth is, though, that Wigan, and not Wakefield, were our biggest enemy on that day to forget ...

We kicked ourselves all the way back home. I don't have any doubts at all that every Wigan fan who had made the trip to London felt like kicking us, too. And I could not have blamed them.

In the eyes of the supporters, there is only one sin bigger than limping home from Wembley without the cup, despite all the cheers for 'gallant losers'. That is having the big pot within your grasp, lifting their hopes sky-high - and then getting mopped up.

This applies in particular to Wigan fans, because they are simply not used to being shown up. Yet there I was - the losing captain in my last two Cup Finals. Once to the well-loathed enemy St Helens, and once to a bunch from Yorkshire that we had had on the floor, then allowed to get up and knock us flat.

It isn't an enviable position to be in ...

So you will understand exactly how I felt when I got my next crack two years later. A chance that placed a double responsibility on me. That of coach and captain, when the long march to Wembley ended in May, 1965, and we were face to face with big Fred Ward's boys from Hunslet.

It was the Final everybody predicted was going to be a pushover ... for Wigan.

That's a laugh. Because this was no pushover. It was the game everybody said would be one way, with Wigan's skill and speed simply swamping Hunslet's forward thrust and limited back power.

There was no swamping done that day. Hunslet put up the grittiest, gamest opposition I have ever encountered.

They pushed us all the way, using their limited skills to the full. They gave me a hatful of frights before we nosed home by 20-16. And at the end I was proud to have played in a wonderful classic.

Let us go back and look at the Final that critics think was the all-time best.

It was the game, as I have said, in which I was not only staking my reputation as a captain and a player, but as a coach as well.

I couldn't help remembering Joe Egan's sudden break with Wigan after St Helens licked us four years earlier.

There was only one plan I could adopt. Go out and make sure that the big, lunging Yorkshire pack was kept under so we could break free and rack up the tries that would count. Again, it was a case of deciding who was the biggest threat, and making sure that the threat didn't get a chance to materialise.

My calculations came up with one answer. Coach and captain Fred Ward had to be taken care of. And quickly.

Ward was the dynamo Hunslet would be relying on to spark them off. But I knew he could be shaken. And I knew that Laurie Gilfedder was the man to do the job.

I was right. Gilfedder got to Ward twice in quick succession, early in the game, and really rattled him with very heavy tackles. Ward still needed SOME watching after that. But not enough to make him a really big nuisance.

Even with Ward reduced to an under-power performer, however, Hunslet still turned on enough heat to give us a pretty sticky time.

At one stage we had forged into a 12-4 lead, and, even though I knew it was never wise to take anything for granted at Wembley, I couldn't help thinking: 'We've got them cold. They are finished.' How wrong I was!

Hunslet had other ideas, centre Geoff Shelton in particular. He shot out of nowhere with a glorious middle-of-the-field burst, was caught just short of the line but managed to slide over for a try under the posts. Bill Langton banged over the goal - and I had to wipe out any cocky thoughts I had had of a stroll-away victory.

The trouble, so far as Hunslet were concerned, was that they couldn't match their attacking spirit with a solid enough defence.

And how grateful I was for that. Particularly after the interval, when they cracked open again, and Gilfedder went crashing over in the corner. I never got a sweeter kick out of landing a goal than I did from the touchline conversion that followed.

Again I could start thinking to myself: 'We really have got them running, this time.' Trevor Lake seemed to be thinking on the same lines as he hared through for his second try, leaving his opposite number John Griffiths behind.

But Hunslet seemed determined to give me no peace of mind. Griffiths hit back - and I must say all the effort he had put into the game made his try fully deserved.

That's the way it stayed to the end. They edged even closer to us with a couple of goals from Langton. And all we could do was hang and stand up to the pounding.

We did it. But I never want to have a shave as close as that again.

Still, that's half the magic of Wembley. You know you are in for a tough time. Only once have I been wrong about that ... in that stroll in the sun that ruined Hull.

I will always remember, and be grateful to teams like Workington, St Helens, Wakefield and Hunslet. They fought like tigers, and that is what you expect. They made it possible for me to snatch my most memorable moments, win or lose.

A hard struggle, in a jewel of a setting like Wembley, makes every bruise and broken bone I have ever collected worthwhile.

And I will say that five times over.

Glory In The Centre Spot

4

INVINCIBLE VINCE

One of the greatest tragedies in Rugby League, during the most important part of my own playing career, is that there were three tremendous players queueing for one single key position in our international team. That vital spot was Number Thirteen. And the loose-forwards to whom I refer? No prizes for an all-correct answer. They are, of course, Vince Karalius (St Helens and Widnes), Derek Turner (Hull K.R., Oldham and Wakefield), and Johnny Whiteley (Hull).

Now I have played both with and against all three. It was, as I have said, a crying shame that we had to have all three hitting their peak at precisely the same period in their outstanding playing days. They 'came' all at the same time. During the next four or five years we might not get another loose-forward in an England Rugby League jersey who is half as good as Vince, Derek or Johnny.

None of 'em would ever let you down. They obeyed playing instructions to the letter. They have all skippered their respective clubs. They have all been members of Guts Incorporated and trotted out some fantastic performances, without any prompting, when under my captaincy.

Whiteley has been the prince of the peerless pass. Turner has always lived up to his nick-name of 'Rocky' and, like myself, has collected that R.L. Challenge Cup on three occasions at Wembley Stadium. Karalius? Well, here's my man. Here's the rampaging, tough-as-teak No. 13 who just gets the Ashton vote over Whiteley and Turner.

Karalius is, and always has been, terrific with an outsize capital T. His ball distribution, on practically every occasion, has equalled that of 'Rocky' Turner's, although Turner always enjoyed a definite advantage in another department. You see, 'Rocky' had one outstanding asset when in his pomp: He could stand back after a play-the-ball and just give that ball the big boot. Its flight would have distance and accuracy. For years and years I've never seen another loose-forward with such a kicking ace up his sleeve.

Karalius doesn't have a kick worth mentioning. But he has everything else - and more besides. He is a king-size player who has given everything he has got into earning that crown. Off the field? Well, Vince, who has reached the summit in self-discipline, is a quiet-spoken, king-size gentleman.

Indeed, this game of ours, claimed to be the toughest in the world, has bred none tougher than my old opponent, one-time team-mate and great pal Karalius. He was called 'The Wild Bull of the Pampas' by Australians who feared his bone-jarring crash-tackles ... but learned to admire and even love him. He is colourful, classy and courageous. He has been the finest loose-forward I have ever seen. Traill, Valentine, Ivison, Turner, Whiteley and Poole have all been outstanding. But the daddy of them all - and especially when the chips are down - has been Karalius.

This craggy-faced, immaculately-proportioned terror of *any* opposition has the biggest pair of hands in the Rugby League business. He also has a heart to match them.

I needed no further proof of this than in that memorable

Invincible Vince

1958 Ashes-winning tour of 'Down Under', when Karalius
waged his own one-man war on those Aussies and brought
them down to size with his immense strength and skill. Later,
in other international matches, and especially when the going
has got really tough, I have only had to turn to Karalius and
say: 'You just start driving that pack along, mate, and I'll have
a bit of a chat with the backs.' The result has always been the
same: Fearless, sledge-hammer play from Vinty, which
spurred his forwards to play above themselves.

Off the field the gentle giant. On it, a firm believer that
there's only one way to play Rugby League football ... the
hard way. Time and again when away on tour I've heard him
expound his theory: 'Make your first tackle the last. Give
your opponent something to think about. Let them know
you are playing.'

Yet Karalius, truly one of the iron men of Rugby League,
has never been known to 'squeal', deliberately kick, or bite
an opposing player. And a spot of biting does occasionally
go on in this game of ours, you know.

Karalius, tackles hard but fairly. If he gives a knock, then
he expects to get one back in return. He is a slightly less
ferocious, but much more mature and cool-headed player
than when he was with St Helens and especially during that
'58 tour of the Commonwealth with the British Rugby
League Lions.

Only recently I was chatting with Vince, who is now
captain of his home-town club, Widnes, and recalled that
tour when he took Australia by storm.

Vince, or Vinty as he is also known, still chuckles over
those cuttings from Australian newspapers, which certainly
pulled no punches in their descriptions of this Number
Thirteen:

'Karalius, by his vigour and octopus-like tackles, does
everything to stir the blood of his opponents ...'

'Karalius believes there's no room for beg pardons in
football ...'

59

'Long-jawed Karalius, "The Wild Bull of the Pampas", is a dedicated wrecker of Australian forwards ...'

'Karalius, a fine footballer, but somewhat hot-headed, gave Skinner and Menzies a torrid day. He bowled them over often before they could even move ...'

'This vigorous, mobile player is one of the most destructive players that England has sent to Australia ...'

'This St Helens boiler-maker with classic tastes in music can stiff-arm tackle to the lilt of *Il Trovatore* ...'

'As he clocks the Kangaroos he probably hums the Toreador song from *Carmen* ...'

That was the build-up Karalius was getting. As he told me at the time: 'Opponents are dead keen to set their stall up against me out here, Eric. I know on this tour I'm a marked man - and that I am going to give and take a lot. I'm determined to show just who is boss in *every* game. I'll shift anybody who tries to stop me.'

Now I have never seen any forward anywhere or at any time be so devastating or pull off such a cruelly efficient demolition job as Vince did in 1958 under that Australian sun.

It was no secret among our party - or among the Kangaroos themselves for that matter - that Karalius always avoided shaking hands with an opposing Australian player before a big game. He never appeared over-anxious to shake their hands in his shovel-sized fist even after a match.

No, Karalius took an awful lot of punishment in that trip 'Down Under'. But he emerged a battle-scarred, unbeaten hero, still the same uncomplaining Vince, quiet-spoken as ever, taking every bump in his stride, and still enjoying a bit of a lark with the boys.

Karalius, who always considered the Aussies to be among the worst set of losers in Rugby League, believed it was two-faced to be hand-shaking like long-lost friends with players who had been spending the previous eighty minutes 'roughing him up'.

'Keep the hand-shakes for players you like and respect,' he used to say. 'Otherwise, it is an empty, meaningless gesture. And that's how it would be if I shook hands with my Australian opponents.'

Concerning his play, Karalius has always drilled his mind right along one particular straight line: He plays it *very* hard, but *never* intentionally dirty. And there's a world of difference between playing it hard and going into a game with the set idea of using dirty, underhand tactics which often, unfortunately, are not detected by either referees or touch-judges.

That brings me to the Dimond versus Karalius incident which earned Vince a three-match suspension and cost him a place in England's line-up for the first Test match in Sydney in 1958, which the Kangaroos won by 25 points to eight.

The suspension came when Karalius was the first of four players to get their marching orders from referee Colin Pearce in our touring side's match against New South Wales. The Lions, leading by only one slender point at the interval, finally ran out 19-10 winners.

Tough? You can say that again .... and again. Karalius was soon being lectured - for stunning N.S.W. player Doug Cameron, who dropped the ball, then followed it on to the pitch a split-second later.

Our skipper, Alan Prescott, told Vince to play it cool for a spell. None of our lads had time, and certainly not Karalius.

No use blaming the Aussies. No use blaming ourselves. The guilt for the tension which reached boiling-point, the over-robust tactics, and all the flare-up, was just about equally shared. That big crowd wasn't helping matters either.

The Karalius incident with N.S.W. star Peter Dimond started the little procession to the dressing-rooms for those 'early baths'.

Glory In The Centre Spot

Karalius went for his after fifty-one minutes' play. Dimond didn't like it when Vince tackled him. There was a spot of retaliation and then - wham! - Dimond was on the deck.

It was alleged that Karalius had kicked Dimond. Rubbish! It was a clout. I know. I saw it.

What was even more disastrous, from Great Britain's point of view, is the farcical, totally unjust punishment meted out to Karalius, compared to the three dismissed Aussie 'offenders'. For Vince, as I have said, was suspended for *three matches* - just enough to keep him out of our international side for that vital forthcoming first Test, which the Lions lost by 25 points to 8 before a crowd of 67,637.

Karalius still claims he was made out to be the real villain of that Great Britain - New South Wales rough-house. I claim he received one of the most biased, unjust punishments it's been my displeasure to recall in international Rugby League football.

About ten minutes after the Karalius dismissal Rex Mossop, the former Leigh, Lancashire, second-row forward, was sent off after stretching me out as I was taking a pass from Eric Fraser (Warrington).

Soon to follow Mossop was his team-mate and stand-off half-back Greg Hawick, dismissed for an incident when he was being tackled by Phil Jackson (Barrow).

The third Aussie player to receive marching orders from referee Pearce was Dimond, for alleged kicking at Mick Sullivan as the Yorkshire-born winger was preparing to tackle him.

Mossop was suspended for one match. Hawich and Dimond were suspended until June 17. The Karalius case was dealt with by the N.S.W. Judiciary Committee *two days after* that game with New South Wales.

Karalius, we all thought, had come in for the rough edge of the stick when the decision dropped like a bomb in our tour party's hotel headquarters. Suspension until June 22 ... just five days more than that received by Dimond, guilty of just the same alleged kicking offence, according to that Judiciary Committee.

It kept Karalius out of the opening Test match, a floodlit game against Brisbane, and also a match against Queensland. It was, as I have emphasised, a thoroughly harsh and disgusting raw deal. Co-manager Tom Mitchell (Workington) described it as 'this unconstitutional penalty', and appealed against it.

Mr Mitchell worded his statement as follows: 'Dimond was found guilty of kicking, yet only received one match. I want to know why the punishment against a British player is three times that give to an Australian sent off for an alleged similar infringement.'

The Tests, which I have discussed in more detail elsewhere in my story, were wide open following our first crushing defeat. Both Karalius and I were absentees from our opening Test flop in the three-match series. So were Dick Huddart and Brian McTigue - a disastrous omission from a selection point of view.

Karalius, mighty Karalius, was out there with a bang in the second Test the R.L. Lions had to win at all costs. It's history now how Alan Prescott and Karalius made this a Great Britain touring side's finest hour in Rugby League history since the 'Rorke's Drift Battle' in 1914, when the British side, down to only ten men at the end, clinched the series in a bloody, bruising, torrid game. It's history now how Prescott told his players, 'Say nowt about it - my arm's broken!' in that Australian sunshine of '58. And it's also history how Karalius, with Wigan's Dave Bolton off with a broken collar-bone, had to leave his lock position and take over the stand-off berth.

Loose-forward or stand-off, it made no difference to invincible Vince. He was really on the rampage. The Aussies threw everything but the kitchen sink at him. He took it all on the chin, gave 'em plenty in return, and finally pulled off a peach of a move with his then St Helens team-mate, Alex Murphy.

Glory In The Centre Spot

It was a 'blinder' and went like this: Murphy shot round the open side of the scrum, went like a bomb, and parted to Karalius. Vince made a splendid short burst and succeeded in drawing like a powerful magnet the Kanagaroos' defence. Murphy was completely unmarked. Karalius whipped the ball back to him with a typically Lancashire-style 'It's all yours, lad' shout. Murphy did the rest with his try.

We levelled the series with that glory-loaded 25 point to 18 win. But five players had to go to hospital - Prescott (broken arm); Bolton (broken collar-bone); Fraser (strained right elbow and burst blood-vessels); Jim Challinor (shoulder injury); Karalius (bruised spine).

Karalius was also involved in an internal spot of bother in that '58 tour. It happened when he was really in the dumps on hearing his fate after the New South Wales game - that three-match suspension which automatically eliminated him from the British team in that first Test.

His big pal on tour, Whitehaven's terrific second-row man, Dick 'Tiger' Huddart, was never far away. Huddart, his room-mate, was right by his side on the evening that suspension announcement was made. Huddart did his best to lift up Vince's spirits. Neither is a big drinker at the best of times. They simply had one or two beers and got into conversation with some Australian Rugby League fans. But they reported back to our hotel H.Q. after the curfew time of 10p.m. imposed by the team management.

Bit early for strapping, grown-up Rugby League players who *never* allow themselves to get out of condition, isn't it? Still, those fitness fanatics, Karalius and Huddart, were carpeted. They told our other co-manager, Mr Bennett Manson, that he could put them on the next plane back home! Of course, he didn't. Good job, too, as events turned out.

Karalius has admitted he lost his temper slightly. He admits there was a curfew and that, no matter how early it was, he and Huddart should have stuck to it. Commonsense prevailed in the end, and the matter was finally ironed-out to the satisfaction of 'Barney' Manson, who was only working to the letter, and Messrs Karalius and Huddart.

A smash-hit! That was Karalius and his Great Britain team-mates in the Test 'decider' at Sydney. The Australians were humiliated - and practically annihilated - by 40 points to 17. A section of the 68,720 crowd threw orange peel and even beer bottles on to the pitch. Karalius turned to winger Sullivan and told him: 'I wish this lot would throw us some proper fruit! I could murder an orange or two in this heat.'

No, I'll never forget big Vince for his shattering, all-round performance in that Commonwealth tour. Skipper Prescott, his arm in a sling, summed it up perfectly when he said, 'Of our players McTigue and Karalius were stars of a fine pack of forwards. Karalius has been a key man in the Tests, and I cannot praise his play highly enough.'

Praise? Karalius has collected more than most in his drama-packed, sometimes controversial, always brilliant career.

Respect? Nothing but that for Karalius, who has been feared and liked in equal measure.

Discipline? As his skipper in international matches I've never had a single moment's trouble with Karalius. He doesn't need telling *anything* twice. Often, he never needed telling anything at all. He always has done what comes naturally to a complete Rugby League footballer who infused crowd-pulling power and fantastic will-to-win determination in his play.

In a nutshell, if you are respected in this game of ours, then you must be a good player. And, I have always found, that player is Vincent Peter Patrick Karalius.

He has never played for himself. He is the perfect team-man. He has never been big-headed. He is the player with the big reputation, who, when given pre-match instructions he might not have liked, has never said: 'I'm Karalius ... you can go and jump in the lake.'

He is his own hardest task-master. From being the once over-enthusiastic loose-forward who sometimes risked dismissal with that famed flat-out vigour, he became the ideal leader and ball artist.

Finally, there's the wisecrack made not so long ago by a player who had been at the receiving end of some fair, but ever so bone-crunching Karalius tackles. He said: 'Put Vince and Cassius Clay in a phone booth, and only one bloke would be stepping out of the wreckage at the end - that's Karalius.'

Yes, I'm pretty pleased to have had the honour of playing alongside - and, indeed, even against - this hell-raiser of a loose-forward.

For Karalius must go into *anybody's* books as one of the all-time greats ... the Gentle Giant with the lot in that No. 13 jersey.

5

THAT BLANK CHEQUE PLAYER

That ace New Zealand half-back and former Warrington coach Ces Mountford once described bouncing Billy Boston as his 'blank cheque man'. And I can't go one better than that.

Now there are a hundred and one reasons why the Boston Two-step Boy has a very special place of honour in the Ashton hall of fame. And the main one is ... because he is Billy Boston, that block-bustin' Brown Bomber of a whirlwind winger.

We'll be darn lucky if ever we see his equal again on our Rugby League scene. We might never see anyone with so much crowd-pulling magic for a three-quarter in either the Union or the professional League codes.

To be perfectly honest, we'll be extremely fortunate if, in our lifetime, there's another Union or League wingman with HALF the power, pace and try-grabbing ability of the Boston who became the top wingman in world Rugby.

No mistake about it. No slip of the pen. I definitely included Union, which has *never* in all its history had another wing three-quarter to touch Boston, who deserted their code for professional pay, honours and glamour at Wigan.

As the complete footballer, Boston is the finest I have ever seen. It would be unfair to compare him with St Helens' spring-heeled Springbok, Tom Van Vollenhoven, or with that Aussie flier, Brian Bevan, when at his best. 'Bev' was a grand winger. 'Voll' still is in the top-bracket in the three-quarter business. But, and here's the differences, Billy can play *anywhere* in the backs.

If I were picking my best team I would name Boston first - and fit the other twelve players in somewhere.

Boston, who has been priceless to Wigan, has been the main man at Central Park for a good number of seasons. A bit of speed has been sapped from his play now. But Wigan know they can't go out and buy another Boston. Because there just isn't one around. As I have hinted, there may not be one for another twenty years or more.

One of Boston's faults - if you can call it that - is that he hasn't always realised just how good he is. He is frequently self-critical when he doesn't need to be. Too often he thinks that unless he is scoring tries there is something wrong. He has had some of his best games and not scored a try. Yet he doesn't appreciate that. For Boston is temperamental about his own displays.

Also, in some respects, Boston can be a lazy player. For he only does just enough. No more and no less. But just enough is good enough for Billy - and often too good for anyone else.

It's a common sight on rugby pitches everywhere: Some players running hell for leather, leaving their opponents way behind. Not with Boston. No, sir. He lets the other fellow chase him.

Furthermore, Boston is a big-match player. Easy-meat opponents rarely interest him, or bring out any of the Boston class.

Off the field we are the firmest of friends. On it, as his centre partner and his skipper, I have said things to Billy B. that could make other players see red. But I always get away with it. For that is the true measure of our friendship. And even a player of Billy's' star-quality knows, like anybody else, that he needs a bit of driving at times. That is one of the reasons why, I suppose, we have shared so much success on the rugby field.

He would, of course, have got there on his own. Yet I like to think that, in a small way, I have given Billy B. a little boost up that popularity poll. And, let's face it, Boston has done the same for me to a certain extent.

Oh, if only Billy boy had realised just how good he really is ... and worked that little bit harder! Then, Rugby League fans everywhere, there would never have been a single thought of comparing him with the Lionel Coopers, the Bevans or the Vollenhovens of this game.

Boston would have stood right out on his own. As it is, many keen Rugby League followers consider Billy to have been *just about the best* when put in the reckoning with that admittedly talented trio.

But, if only he had fully grasped that he was the tops, then Boston would have been just that. No danger. As it is, Billy despite his enviable, tremendous make-up, has had that small but vital cog missing from the football machine that could have made all others look in need of an overhaul and greasing.

It was on October 10, 1964, when Boston passed another milestone in his illustrious career - by scoring his 500th try in Wigan's match against Barrow at Central Park.

We won by the handsome margin of 49 points to nil, Billy B. bagging four tries in all.

I'm glad I had a hand in providing him with his 500th trip across the line. It was more of an old pals act than anything else.

I had sprinted through a gap in the Barrow defence. I

could have scored a try myself ... or sent Ray Ashby, our full-back, through for a walk-in try. Instead, I looked around and just waited for Boston to thunder up with one of his old-time bursts, slipped him the pass, and stood by and watched him gallop over near the post.

It was thirty years earlier - on August 6, 1934, to be precise - that this star called William John Boston had been born in a terraced house in Cardiff's dockland area of Tiger Bay.

Jack Winstanley, a journalist on the local newspaper at Wigan, has seen Boston in action on more occasions than any other Rugby League writer.

And Winstanley puts it this way: 'Once in a lifetime an outstanding, unforgettable personality is thrust under the glaring spotlight of sport. Joe Louis reigned supreme in the boxing world. Stanley Matthews became the wizard of soccer, and Len Hutton was the knight of cricket in his time. To Rugby League football came ... Billy Boston.

'Boston is the dusky-skinned kid from Tiger Bay, who strode majestically into his own spotlight of sport from the obscurity of a family of thirteen to fame wherever Rugby League is played. His extraordinary ability as a complete, natural player has made his name know beyond the Rugby League boundaries, too.

'Recently a Wigan boy went proudly to Buckingham Palace to receive an award from the Duke of Edinburgh. Prince Philip opened the conversation by asking: "How is Billy Boston getting on at Wigan?"

'Almost as soon as the school gates had closed behind him Boston was playing for a leading Welsh Rugby Union club - a boy among men. He was a rugby phenomenon in a land where Rugby is a legend.

'There is not the slightest doubt he would have taken international Rugby Union by storm, for his ability went beyond question. But the red jersey of Wales was not to be his; the professional scouts from the North saw to that.

70

'Rugby League's biggest player-hunt started when Boston was only sixteen years old, and by the time he was eighteen, any one of half a dozen clubs would have sunk deep into their coffers to have him on their books. It is history now that Wigan succeeded where so many others had failed in persuading him to become a professional footballer.

'His memorable years with Wigan started on a Friday the Thirteenth in March, 1953, when he scrawled his valuable signature on the professional ticket that was to bring him a small fortune in money, all the honours open to a Rugby League player, and some bitter heartaches.

'Boston electrified Services Rugby Union before bursting sensationally into the Rugby League world. Transferred, not by accident, to the Royal Signals at Catterick, Yorkshire, he became the star of a side which challenged and beat most of the cream of R.U. talent of this country.

'In his first match, just one day after arriving at Catterick, he had spectators gasping as he scored *thirty-seven* points himself. In another game he scored eight tries. when the Royal Signals won the Army Cup in March, 1953, he accounted for six of his side's eight tries. In a full season of Army Rugby Union he amassed the mammoth total of 126 tries. And he was still only eighteen.

'When Boston made his Rugby League debut in Wigan's second team, special posters were displayed to announce that he would be playing. A crowd of 8,500 came to see him. And even the Wigan spectators, the most sophisticated crowd in the game, saw straight away that here, indeed, was a shining star. But for all their shrewdness, they could hardly have imagined that a few weeks later, after only *six* Rugby League matches, Boston was to win the game's highest honour - an Australian tour with the aristocracy of Britain's professional Rugby.

'The boy from Tiger Bay had taken his first step on the ladder of sporting fame. In a few short weeks his exciting brilliance had taken him to a peak which no other player had reached so quickly. Boston was the first coloured Rugby League player chosen for a British tour of Australasia, and he made just as big an impact on Australian and New Zealand crowds as he had done in Britain.

'He still knew next to nothing about the rudiments of the game when he left England's shores, but once again his great natural talent carried him from one success to another. He broke the Tour try-scoring record at his first attempt.'

Let us glance back, for a moment, at what this prolific scorer did on his first trip away from Britain - and the professional club he had only just joined.

He had gone out there in 1954 with three other Wigan players: Ernie Ashcroft (vice-captain of the tour party), Jack Cunliffe and Nat Silcock.

He scored thirty-six tries in eighteen matches - and in five of these he failed to score. His highest bag of tries was six against Northern New South Wales. Yet his best solo performance was surely the scoring of four tries in the first Test against New Zealand.

And this is how one of Australia's top sports writers summed up that '54 Tour which really belonged to Boston:

'This Welsh coloured boy is potentially the greatest Rugby League winger the world has produced. He was unquestionably the outstanding success of the 1954 English team's tour of Australia. He scored 25 tries in Australia, while he got four tries in the first Test against New Zealand.

'In the combined tour of Australia and New Zealand Boston has set up a try-scoring record which completely dwarfs the performances of such past great wingers as Alf Ellaby, John Ring, Stanley Smith and Tom Danby.

'Boston has developed on the tour. He is six-feet tall and now weighs 14 stones 2 lbs. of bone and muscle. He has good pace in his long, raking strides; a sidestep off either foot; a shoulder and a hip. In Australia he developed one of the most vicious fends (hand-off) I have ever seen.'

Three years later this sensational wingman was back in Australia for the World Cup Series. And, shortly afterwards, for this 'best in the world' winger, came his first experience of colour prejudice.

The Great Britain party broke their homeward trip in South Africa, where they played three exhibition games. The South African organisers emphasised that if Boston did accompany the British team to their country, then he would have to live apart from his team-mates, eating and sleeping at different hotels. This, they stated, would have to be enforced under the rules of segregation.

Well, I know that Billy had decided against going to South Africa before he even left England. Yet he wasn't so happy about the programmes published for those exhibition matches. They contained photographs of every member of the Great Britain World Cup party ... every member, that is, except Billy Boston.

Thank goodness, the same problem does not exist on our playing pitches over here. Think of St Helens' Vollenhoven and their other winger Len Killeen, to mention but a couple of South African Rugby League stars who bring credit to our game. Boston has played against them often, is friendly with them, and I know the admiration is mutual.

One of Boston's best-ever international displays was again in Australia - this time, in the second Test at Brisbane, on June 30, 1962, when Billy B. scored two tries.

Great Britain won by 17 points to 10 to retain the Ashes and become the first side since 1928 to win the first two Tests in Australia. Our team had absolutely wiped the pitch with the Kangaroos in the first Test at Sydney, winning by the overwhelming margin of 31 points to 12.

Eddie Waring described the second Test as follows: 'Australia's plan to stop Billy Boston at all costs bounced right back in their red faces at Brisbane. The beefy pride of Wigan crashed his way through for two vital tries that made sure of the Ashes staying with Britain.

Glory In The Centre Spot

'The Aussies had thought they could sew up this second Test and square the rubber by slapping the shackles on bouncing Billy. So they sent over a stream of high kicks for Boston to field, hoping to hammer him into the ground in the process.

'It was the Aussies who had the hammering. The Wigan walloper took everything they gave and repaid it with dividends. In fact, this fit, powerful Boston has never played better on the tour.'

Joe Egan, ex-Wigan and present Widnes coach, goes along with me in stressing that Boston could have been an even finer player than he is already.

Joe, who certainly knows his players when he sees 'em, has gone on record as saying: 'Although I haven't seen a more complete footballer than Boston, I consider he could have been even better. He would have done even greater things had he possessed a "killer instinct". But he is always too bothered about the other fellow.'

Egan claims that Boston is the most perfect rugby player he has ever seen. 'If Wigan had paid £30,000 for him he would have been worth it,' said Joe. 'Wigan have had their money's-worth. He is the sort of player I would like to sign - because he has everything a rugby player needs.

Speaking in general terms, not just as Widnes' coach, Billy could play in my team in any position except the front row.

'Yet Boston should, at times, have been more keen on creating personal records. If he had set his mind to it, he could have broken Brian Nordgren's Wigan record of sixty-four tries in one season without much trouble. But personal records don't bother him particularly. That's his make-up.'

Finally, there's that 'blank cheque' assessment from that famous Kiwi and former Wigan half-back Ces Mountford: 'Given a blank cheque, and all the players of the Rugby League to choose from, which one would you go for as the most complete footballer and the most useful man to have in your side?

'At club, international or world-class levels, there are plenty of players in the modern game to match up to any in a previous era. With unlimited cash and the chance to sign anyone, I would be spoiled for choice.

'As a start, I could think of the specialists - men of one or two positions. Forwards like Vince Karalius, Brian McTigue, Johnny Whiteley and Derek Turner.

'I could think of backs like the supreme Alex Murphy; wingers like Tom Vollenhoven, Brian Bevan, Mick Sullivan, Frank Carlton and Ike Southward; centres like Jim Challinor, Neil Fox, Alan Buckley and Eric Ashton. All value for a lot of money.

'But the man I think I would have - because he can do more things better than any other player in the game - is Wigan's Billy Boston.

'If I bought Billy I think I would have a man of so many trades that I would be certain to get my money's-worth. There may be better faster men than Billy over half the length of the field, and there are certainly heavier men. But no one has a better weight-speed ratio than Billy.

'The "Voll" is obviously a great winger, the finest over a distance with a chance. But Boston at short range is the better man for upsetting the tight-set defence. Boston has swerve and, for his bulk, a remarkably tight sidestep. He takes the good or the awkward ball, the long or the short flip of a pass far better than any other winger. He can play an excellent game on either wing, at centre or stand-off.

'On attack, Boston can use all his weight, or waft through with the grace of a ballet dancer. He can, too, hurl that huge bulk on the shortest way to the line and score through sheer, shattering strength. Obviously he has courage. He never shirks "having a go", however forlorn the hope.

'On defence, Boston can have the effect of a flying bomb. It needs a lot of courage when Billy is unleashed - that 's the word - to take man and ball fairly, but with such a bone-shaking tackle. I think Boston has taken the ginger out of star back opposition more often than any other man in the game.

'Boston has speed and weight. He is a match-winner from forlorn hopes. He is a man of many parts in defence and attack - and a man of many positions.

'Yes, I would have Billy Boston first for my cash. With his signature, I would solve any back worry ... and I would have a top forward ready for the pack in his declining years.'

Well, those were your words, Ces, shortly before you returned to your native New Zealand. You said it first. And, as I pointed out earlier in my story, I cannot go one better than your pen-portrait of my wing partner and off-the-field pal, Wigan's own Billy B.

6

ALEXANDER THE GREAT

Genius - real genius that explodes in your face and leaves you groping dazedly for the right words - is rare in Rugby League as it is in any business worth the name.

Yet, in the 1965-66 season, the Great Britain selectors tossed aside for a spell the man who is probably the only genuine, undeniable genius they could have had in the first Test against the New Zealanders.

And when that happened another sad little line was added to the case history of the most baffling, infuriating and brilliant enigma I have run into in eleven tough years of club and Test warfare.

The case history of a man called Murphy. Alex Murphy, the whiz kid from St Helens. Murphy, the terrier with a tongue that won't keep still. Murphy, the prancing, dancing tearaway I look at and envy.

Yes, envy is the right word. Because even after collecting every honour that this game can hand out, I will admit candidly: I wish I was as good as Murphy is.

But I will also admit, I wasn't staggered when the

selectors decided they could do without The Saint.

Well, I don't pretend to know everything that goes on in the minds of the Test selectors. They have come up with some strange ones for as long as I have been around. I suppose they will again.

One thing can never be denied - on playing ability alone, Murphy commands an automatic place in any team, any time, any place.

I didn't exactly choke on my cornflakes, however, when I heard Alex had been 'axed' for the Test series opener at Swinton, when the scrum-half job went to Tommy Smales (Bradford Northern). Because, in all the times I have been fearing, admiring, sometimes cursing, and all too often chasing Murphy, he himself has been the biggest single enemy of little Alexander Murphy.

There isn't any doubt that he will go down as one of the all-time great half-backs. If you like you can throw in Tommy Bradshaw, Gerry Helme, and any of the others. If they were better - and I never met them in their prime - they must have been out of this world.

I have heard people compare Alex to that brilliant soccer player, Denis Law. They say that Denis isn't half the menace when he puts a rein on his fiery temperament. Well, maybe that is true of Denis Law. I don't believe, however, that it is one hundred per cent true of Murphy.

Luckily, in his own way, Alexander the Great has a bit of respect for me. He has usually stayed out of trouble when I have been around.

Alex, though, would probably grin a little and scoff a lot if I dared to mention respect to him. Respect is something he can manage without, thank you, when he steps into the swirling, temper-popping heat of a game.

His theory is simple: There is nobody on this field who is better than I am. So why respect any of them?

There is something that happened one torrid day at St Helens in 1960. A vital match ... a match needing all the rapid-fire thinking and searing speed that 'Mister Magic' Murphy can produce as easily as switching on a light.

But what happened? He was involved in an 'incident' with Wigan's Mick Sullivan. And both players got their marching orders from the referee.

Stupid people said after that little episode that Wigan had put Sullivan in there against Murphy deliberately to provoke him. In effect, to get him sent off. That, of course, is just sheer nonsense. The only provocation Alex got on that day was his own urge to go in and sort things out.

I'm not going to say that Murphy doesn't wind up on the receiving end of a whole lot of provocation. Rugby League is a ruthless and highly competitive affair. You play to win - and you don't win if the best man the opposition have is given a mile of rope to wander around on.

Alex is a marked man in every game he plays. If you are as good as he is you have to accept that is going to happen. But don't let anyone tell you that he can't take care of himself. He is a remarkably strong, tough and tenacious little character. But with the match-winning reputation he has, it would be a full-time job making sure the 'assassins' don't succeed, without actually nosing his way into more grief.

Murphy's 'To-hell-with-'em' shortage of respect isn't anything that has come on suddenly Or something that has developed as his skills have built up to legendary proportions.

It has always been there. It was there in the days I knew him as a wisecracking teenager enjoying a Sunday night drink with me before the 'pictures' in St Helens.

Even then Alex, the former schoolboy sensation everyone knew would write new greatness into the game, was firmly convinced that he was going to be the best ...and the rest had better watch out. He was so right.

The open unquenchable confidence was there when he rocketed on to the Australian tour at the age of seventeen, while his contemporaries were picking their way carefully through their apprenticeship, and worrying over whether they would stay the course.

He was supposed to be the 'baby' of the side. Some baby! The old hands kidded him: 'You are coming up against Keith Holman, one of the best there is. You'll learn a lot.'

And Alex cracked back without a smile: 'It's Holman who is coming up against me. He might do a bit of learning.'

Again ... he was right. They broke about even in the first Test. Not bad, they said, for a 17-year-old kid. They were saying a whole lot more than that after Alex had finished with Holman in the second Test at Brisbane.

He gave the old Aussie fox one heck of a run-around. Holman was groggy at the end of it. And maybe he did learn something from Murphy. Because there was plenty to learn!

We won that game, even though Alan Prescott broke an arm and we were down to eleven men. And nobody called Alex the 'baby' any more.

Oh, yes, Alex is right down the list when it comes to respecting anybody. He doesn't make any apology for it. I still wince over a classic he dropped in a bar in Australia, two nights before a country game. Just a simple game, a run-out with nothing at stake. But when Alex is playing, he reckons there is always something at stake.

We were talking and one of the 'locals' just chipped in and told us he was the father of the full-back who would be playing against us. I never met a man who was so proud of his son ... until Alex announced dryly: 'I'll give him my regards every time I go past him!'

The man's chin dropped down to his chest. I never saw a man so hurt. He never said another word all night. Alex? He didn't think he had said a word out of place. And, what was more, he proceeded to do exactly what he had said he would do.

The Aussie crowds simply love Alex, even when he is handing out lessons to the likes of Keith Holman.

Perhaps it is because, Down Under, they genuinely adore a scrapper. Nobody ever accused Alex of not being a 100-per-cent fighter.

English crowds aren't as ready to forgive him. I believe that Alex is soundly hated on at least two-thirds of the grounds in the Rugby League. Hated to a pitch that is reserved especially for him.

Like any genius - and I will never apologise for using that word when I am talking about Murphy - he suffers from the jealousy of the opposition.

After all, what crowd likes to see its idols made to look second-rate? Alex does just that with casual, almost monotonous regularity. And what is more - he makes it absolutely clear that he is enjoying every tormenting minute of it.

Furthermore, there is another side to Murphy's make-up. He has now developed a bit of a persecution complex about referees. I can't count the number of times he has moaned to me: 'That man doesn't like me.'

What surprises me about a reaction like that from Alex is the very fact that he is surprised himself. After all, he doesn't exactly go out of his way to endear himself to referees.

Outspoken. That's Murphy, who had this to say about himself in an article he wrote for a local newspaper way back in August, 1961:

'I'm no angel and I approach this Rugby League game on a give-and-take basis, expecting punishment and freely admitting that I am by no means the most even-tempered fellow on earth.

'It's a tough game, needing tough men to play it properly, with no room at the top for what the fans call the 'chicken hearts'.

'But I'm no fool, either, and I don't go looking for trouble. I strongly disagree with those who claim I do. They say this because I don't stand any nonsense from the big forwards who want to push the little chaps like myself around all the time.

'There is a world of difference between a back who sticks up for himself and won't be pushed around, and the one who is foolish enough to set out to antagonise the big forwards. I stick up for myself and my rights, but I'm not daft enough to start baiting the giants of the pack who could eat me in a straight fight.

'If the other fellows will just let me play football I'll never be in trouble. Yet it's a lot to expect a player to take all with a smile when the softening-up boys get going.

'Call me hot-headed Murphy if you wish. But this is the truth ... I want to get on with the game. And I'm no worse than the next fellow when it comes to rough stuff when I am left alone.

'Perhaps I'm sometimes too quick to flare up, but how would you feel if you were flattened to the ground and then had one man rubbing your nose, another prodding around your eyes, and a third experimenting with your ear to see how far it will stretch?

'It takes a far more even-tempered player than myself to go through this sort of treatment without feeling a very strong urge to retaliate.

'I really do try to keep myself off the boil, but it's difficult when operating in the middle of the field, where the big forwards have a better chance of getting their hands on a player.

'I realise, of course, that many St Helens fans have my own interests at heart when they say, "Don't go asking for trouble".

'They think I will get myself sent off. That's the last thing I want to happen, and I am constantly trying to keep cool. It's tough, however, for the smaller man who refuses to be bullied off the game.

'I do my utmost to keep out of trouble, but it is often forced on me. I must repeat that I am not squealing, and that

I am no more an angel than anybody else in the game.'

Finally, there is the skill, the sheer baffling, brilliant skill, of this man Murphy. Almost too much of it to be wrapped up in one man.

It is enough to make me fear Murphy more than any other opponent I have ever come up against in Rugby League.

I fear him because he thinks faster than any other player I know.

I fear him because, with one twist of his body, one burst of fantastic acceleration, he can turn a lost cause into a triumph.

I fear him most of all because nothing he ever does can be predicted. And a man you can't plan against is a nightmare.

But if I was given the chance to have a nightmare playing alongside me, I would say every time: Make mine Murphy. And I will take a chance on his outspokenness.

Glory In The Centre Spot

7

MAC THE KNIFE

Big Norman Provan, the assassin of the Antipodes, was stomping and snorting on the warpath. Which, if you have never seen this hulking Aussie hell-bent on a streak of destruction, I can tell you is not an engaging sight.

When Provan hit the trouble trail - and that was often - you had three alternatives. You either moved, got moved, or put a very big strain on your ability to stand up in front of a runaway truck.

And suddenly it happened. There was Provan, lying sweet, low, and oh, so silent, on the crisp green turf of the Sydney Cricket Ground. Out to the world, and just about as much of a menace as a baby on christening day.

I have watched an army of men get mad, and a lot more get flattened because of it, all the way from Wigan to Wagga Wagga. So what makes that one jolting, jarring collision stay sharply in my mind?

Simple. The man who had slammed Provan, the master terrorist, into that prone and docile state was Brian McTigue. 'Mighty Mac'... 'Mac the Knife' ... 'The Wordless Wonder.'

The big, homely miner, who would make a mile-long detour to avoid being cruel to a gnat.

Any one of those nicknames will tell you why that swift and efficient piece of mayhem in the Sydney sunshine still makes me shake my head with wonder. It was the one and only time I have seen McTigue shake off the placid mask of long-suffering reason - and lash out in anger.

And that, more than anything else, is why McTigue ranks in my memory as probably the greatest all-round forward - and certainly the greatest all-round man - I have played behind.

More than the sure, unhurried and thoughtful ball-handling that have carved and made easy countless tries for Wigan and for Great Britain.

More than the slamming, but never dirty, tackles that have wrecked just as many chances for the men who had the bad luck to meet him head on.

The never-complaining, no-excuses outlook - the sheer professionalism of McTigue - outranks all of these when you start adding up the qualities that have made him The Best.

And yet, it is this very solid silence that has stopped Brian from leaving behind an even deeper and more lasting mark on the game. The mark of the truly great pack-leader, the lifter of other players to heights they didn't dream they could reach.

For Brian will never, on the field or off it, encourage, shout at, praise or advise the men he is playing with. When I have told him about this, tried to squeeze some noise out of him, he has always replied tersely: 'If I have to tell them what to do, they have no right to be playing for Wigan.'

Now that is just fine. Until you realise that McTigue is in a class all by himself. That he is the man the others would follow blindly ... and not go far wrong.

I have described that other great, Alex Murphy, as the man who lets himself down by talking too much. McTigue - the other name that spells M for Murder to the opposition - is, if anything, the man who doesn't talk enough.

McTigue is never a joker when he is playing. He is much too good for that, and there isn't a team or a coach around that doesn't know it. Away from the action, though? Well, Brian's strong silent act gets a load of laughs. It has become a sort of by-word in the game, but Brian just grins and shrugs it off.

Take the time in New Zealand, in 1958, when the touring team was offered a free trip by an airline over the exotic Rotorua thermal region. Brian, to the surprise of absolutely no one, ducked out, and went off somewhere by himself. And, sure enough, this cryptic little line appeared in the airline's visitors' book next day: 'Brian McTigue missed out again.'

Brian just wasn't interested in looking at the sights. He was a sort of father figure in the party, and that kind of thing was for the youngsters.

But maybe Dick Huddart, on one of the tours, summed him up best of all: 'McTigue is crazy - like a fox.'

Like most men to whom a big mouth is the cardinal sin, McTigue is amazingly tough. I still get a twinge of second-hand pain when I think of what happened to him after a league match at Hull, in 1956. Brian was cut pretty badly between the eyes. Next day, his face was swollen like a pumpkin. It must have been giving him hell - and we found out it was because a bad stitching job had been done on it.

But McTigue never bleated once. I reckon I am a pretty easy-going character. But if it had happened to me, I know I would have been out gunning for that doctor. Not Mac, however, for he just grinned, then moaned a bit because he would have to miss a game or two.

Maybe the roots of McTigue's calm acceptance of pain, and his grim determination not to lose his temper, are buried deep in his past. In the days before he stepped into Rugby League as a substitute for the Giants' Hall Colliery side in Wigan.

In the days when he was a good enough boxer to be

ranked among Britain's top ten light-heavyweights, box exhibitions with world champion Joey Maxim, and get an offer from the American to go back to the States with him.

Brian doesn't like to talk much about his boxing career. He got out after his manager was killed in an accident - and as far as he was concerned that was the end of that. I think, too, that he doesn't want people to think he was a trained fighter, in case they ever get the idea he's a man who would throw his weight about just because he has the edge in thumping skill.

Yet, as I said, Norman Provan, the Aussie tough boy, found out sharply and painfully that it doesn't pay to push McTigue's patience all that far.

Mac was even more silent than usual after that Test. I think, in a funny way, he was a bit ashamed that he had let his feelings show through for long enough to clout someone.

But in a game as fiery, rugged and professional as this, even the gentlest men hit trouble at least once. It happened to Brian at Leeds in 1957. He had a bit of a scuffle with Leeds hooker Simms. And the Rugby League world was stunned to hear that McTigue had been sent off. Again, Mac was stiff and silent about the whole thing. But he has said to me plenty of times since: 'I have been sent off twice in my life. And that was for doing nothing.'

A forward with the skills and eight-minute menace of McTigue has every shred of sympathy I can muster. Every game is a battle. Every game makes him more of a marked man. Let's be honest. If I were the coach of a side that had to face him my first instructions would be: 'Get rid of McTigue.' And I wouldn't be too particular how it was done.

Mac knows this, and accepts it. That, to him, is an essential part of the game. And, in a way, I think he is secretly flattered that they should think enough about him to want to 'murder' him.

When McTigue isn't being hunted - and when he isn't leading the hunters an embarrassing dance - he is usually being honoured. And that, for Mighty Mac is the worst part of it all. He ducks away from praise and publicity with a slickness that belies his bulkiness. But it catches up with him, anyway. A man as good as that just can't avoid it.

Mac, I am convinced, would sooner face Vince Karalius a dozen times a day than go through the ordeal they pushed on to him after the Challenge Cup win over Hull in 1959. Much to his dismay, they awarded him the Lance Todd Trophy.

I say dismay, because I have never seen a man suffer so much as Mac did as he counted off the days to the dinner at which the old Salford 'Red Devils' would present him with the award. 'What the hell am I going to say to them?' he moaned. 'Why can't they just send it to me?'

There was no escape. Brian had to get up and face them. And after all that sweating, all he could manage was something like 'Thank you' ... a blush ... and a sharp return to his seat.

No, banqueting halls are not the place for Mac. Speeches are not his meat. The pomp that goes with greatness has been, for him, the most painful part of his fourteen-year career.

But McTigue doesn't need pomp. Nobody needs to be told he is good. He has proved it and he hasn't left behind one glimmer of doubt. He is still proving it today, even though they started writing him off as long as three years ago.

You don't write off a true great as easily as that. Take our cup win over St Helens last season. It opened up the path for our final victory over Hunslet - the game they said was the best Wembley had ever seen. And who made clearing that toughest hurdle against Saints possible? McTigue, naturally.

He did it in one concentrated flash of fire that lit up that grim February day, ducking and bursting through four tackles to send Roy Evans over under the posts to break the 2-2 deadlock.

I have never been more relieved to see his brawny,

bustling frame smash into the heart of the opposition. And I remember murmuring to myself: 'That's some going for a "has-been".'

To me, McTigue will never be a "has-been". True, the crafty old bull, at thirty-five, has slowed down. Maybe, now, he doesn't squeeze out of a tackle as cutely and as often as he did when he was barn-storming across Australia and leaving the Aussies to collect the wreckage.

Perhaps the end isn't too far away. But I know this, McTigue will realise when it has arrived. He will get out, quietly and correctly. He will probably get tongue-tied over saying 'Good-bye'.

And he will leave behind one heck of a big gap.

8

MY WORLD TEAM

I have lost count of the times Rugby League fans have asked me to name the thirteen players I would put into my best-in-the-world team.

A difficult task, in a way. But, for the record, I have chosen only Rugby League footballers who I have played with or against during my own spell in this great game. That means since 1955 - and, therefore, automatically excludes some former outstanding players who had packed up the game, or, if they'll pardon me for being blunt, were 'over the hill' in top-grade rugby.

Here are the players who have been the tops - and at their peak - while I have been around on the Rugby League scene.

Full-back:	Glyn Moses (St Helens);
Right-wing:	Billy Boston (Wigan),
Right-centre:	Reg Gasnier (Australia),
Left-centre:	Neil Fox (Wakefield Trinity),
Left-wing:	Mick Sullivan (Huddersfield, Wigan, St Helens, York and Dewsbury);

Stand-off:	George Menzies (New Zealand),
Scrum-half:	Alex Murphy (St Helens);
Prop forward:	Bill Wilson (Australia),
Hooker:	Ian Walsh (Australia),
Prop forward:	Brian McTigue (Wigan),
Second-row:	Brian Edgar (Workington),
Second-row:	Kel O'Shea (Australia),
Loose-forward:	Vince Karalius (St Helens and Widnes).

Now for a few words about each player and why I have picked him ...

Firstly, there's Moses at full-back. A real good 'un. For all-round attacking ability - and hitting a man fair and square - there has been no one to touch him in that No. 1 jersey, either at club or international level, since the day I first made the senior team at Wigan.

Wingman Boston? Well, he picks himself. And I don't think there will be any arguments either!

Australia's Gasnier just gets my right-centre three-quarter vote over Phil Jackson (Barrow). Simply because Reg can really turn on the gas. He is one of the most elusive centres - and definitely the fastest - I have ever seen. To me, Gasnier always seems to have the amazing knack of doing the wrong thing at the right time ... and it comes off, too.

I will never forget a fantastic piece of work - you can also call it sheer cheek - Gasnier pulled off in the third and final England v. Australia Test at Wigan in 1959.

Gasnier came away like a bullet from his own '25'. Pursuit, once Reg had got his roller-skates on, wasn't much use. Now 'Gas' had Brian Carlson alongside him as he came nearer to our full-back, Wakefield's Gerry Round.

Round, like every other full-back in a similar, unenviable situation, just had to go for the man with the ball. A Gasnier pass to Carlson just before the tackle was on the cards. But was it?

No, Gasnier came right up to Round - then 'dummied' him to the surprise of everybody, players and spectators alike. It was only then that he passed to Carlson, who touched down. Now that's genius ... plus nerve ... plus luck.

So we come to Neil Fox. He's there because of his supreme strength, his goal-kicking prowess, and because, as a big-match player, he can run straight through the Rugby League football alphabet from A to Z. In fact, on the '62 Australasian tour we went together like lumps of sugar in the same tea-cup. I couldn't have asked for a more efficient partner in the middle.

Fox has the ideal build, temperament and skill for a centre. He is one of three rugby-playing brothers. He landed five goals in our opening Test on June 9, 1962, at Sydney, which Great Britain won by 31 points to 12 points. He kicked three more in the second Test, twenty-one days later, which we won by 17 points to 10 at Brisbane.

Sandwiched between these triumphs was Great Britain's overwhelming 47-14 win over North Queensland, in which Fox was on target with seven goals and scored two tries in the bargain.

Any more proof needed? Well, there are these random milestones in the exceptional career of Neil Fox ... 184 goals and 30 tries in the 1961-62 season; 148 goals in 1958-59; 124 goals and 32 tries in 1957-58. And in Wakefield Trinity's 1962 Wembley Final win over Huddersfield Fox landed three goals, notched a try, and won the Lance Todd Memorial Award for the best individual performance.

Over to Mick Sullivan, that much-travelled, hard-as-granite winger who held a Test record-breaking place from 1954 until 1962. Now 'Sully' was terrific with a capital T in international rugby. Ironically, he has had bad games in club football, yet always managed to come off in internationals. A prolific try-scorer and a difficult-to-stop wingman, 'Sully' was absolutely fearless in defence and attack, possessing the guts of Duggie Greenall, some of the side-step trickery of

Glory In The Centre Spot

Brian Bevan, and, at his pomp, only a fraction below the pace of Van Vollenhoven.

The player for the big occasion. That was Sullivan. I still shudder when I think of some of his masterly, power displays 'Down Under'. And they don't come any tougher than in Australia.

Most difficult job has been picking my number one stand-off half-back. My vote just goes to New Zealand's George Menzies. So he edges out even Dave Bolton (Wigan), Ray Price (Warrington) and Brian Clay (Australia). He shook me rigid - and had me gasping in admiration - with the two magnificent tries he scored at Sydney Cricket Ground in 1957 in the World Cup Series. Menzies has made three tours of this country, is extremely hard and rugged for a stand-off and a good, first-time tackler of the old school.

For my perfect scrum-half, in case you haven't guessed it, you just dial M for Murphy. More often than not, that 'M' has also spelt murder for the opposition.

My no. 8 front-row forward? Well, this is going to look funny to some; but my choice would be Australia's Billy Wilson. He was a teak-tough, 'You can have it anywhere, any place, and any time' forward. If you've been on the receiving end of some of his handiwork, as I have been, then you'll appreciate my admiration for his courage, strength and unusual ball-handling skill.

Another Aussie, this time Ian Walsh, of New South Wales, gets the hooking berth. Yes, I would just give him preference over Bob Dagnall (St Helens) and Bill Sayer (Wigan). For one big reason: Walsh, one of Australia's best-ever combinations of hooker and forward, is the finest overall, consistent possession-grabber I have seen. Moreover, his play in the loose is of the highest standard.

My No. 10 in the front row is, of course, Wigan's McTigue. And, I ask you, can *you* name his equal in world Rugby League in the past ten or eleven years?

Cumbrian Brian Edgar, to some, would be another shock

choice. This time in his best position - the one where he really made his name - in the second-row of the pack.

Edgar, a buddy of mine both on and off the international scene, was one of the youngest players ever to feature in a Wembley Challenge Cup Final. He was eighteen years and four months old when he turned out against Barrow in 1955.

He made a firm impression on our Australian tour, and was magnificent 'Down Under' in '62. For Edgar is the ideal tourist. He rarely moans about anything, and never complained when taken out of the second row and shoved up front as a prop.

Brian is one of the few forwards - especially for such a big 'un - who possesses a nifty sidestep. He handles slickly, runs well with the ball, could stop a bus with his hand-off and tackles like a demon. You can't give any more praise than that to a player who tips the scales at almost sixteen stone.

Fourth Australian in my ideal line-up is Kel O'Shea. The impression he made on me in the 1958 tour is summed-up in one word ... TREMENDOUS.

Who else but Karalius at loose-forward? A lone wolf. A fiend for fitness. A classy and courageous player. A No. 13 with the 'killer instinct'. Call him Vince or Vinty. Call him what you like. To me, he has always been THE BEST.

Moreover, anyone who has seen the film of that epic '58 Test match at Brisbane will have to give me full marks for a shrewd choice.

Did someone mention a 'shadow' team ... a second-choice thirteen? Well, I've got it all ready right here:

Full-back:	Brian Carlson (Australia);
Right-wing:	Tom Van Vollenhoven (St Helens),
Right-centre:	Phil Jackson (Barrow),
Left-centre:	Jean Merquey (France),
Left-wing:	Brian Bevan (Warrington);
Stand-off:	Ray Price (Warrington),

Glory In The Centre Spot

Scrum-half:	Keith Holman (Australia);
Prop-forward:	Alan Prescott (St Helens),
Hooker:	Bill Sayer (Wigan and St Helens),
Prop-forward:	Brian Davies (Australia),
Second-row:	Dick Huddart
	(Whitehaven and St Helens),
Second-row:	Derek Turner
	(Hull K.R., Oldham and Wakefield Trinity),
Loose-forward:	Johnny Raper (Australia).

That full-back spot? Well, I know that Carlson hit the headlines as a winger, but it was in the World Cup where he shone as a full-back. And, brother, how he shone!

I know some Rugby League fans would plump for Clive Churchill, or even Wigan's Martin Ryan or Jack Cunliffe. But they were past their best when I ventured into the Rugby League game.

Springbok Vollenhoven was an easy choice. I doubt if anyone - certainly not down Knowsley Road way! - will quibble with that.

Karalius, his former skipper at St Helens, puts it this way: 'There have been some sad misfits from South Africa to our Rugby League game. Many have been called, but few have been chosen. There have been exceptions, of course. Exceptions like Jan Prinsloo ... and Fred ("Punchy") Griffiths ... and Vollenhoven.

'Vollenhoven owes a debt to his inside man in those early days when he was finding his feet in British Rugby League - and that player is Duggie Greenall.

'But now Vollenhoven, the biggest winger of them all from South Africa, has become the maestro of try-scoring "off his own bat".

'He has fantastic speed. He is a clean and good-tempered player. He is one of the finest natural footballers I have ever seen. He has a fantastic knack of being able to do his wing

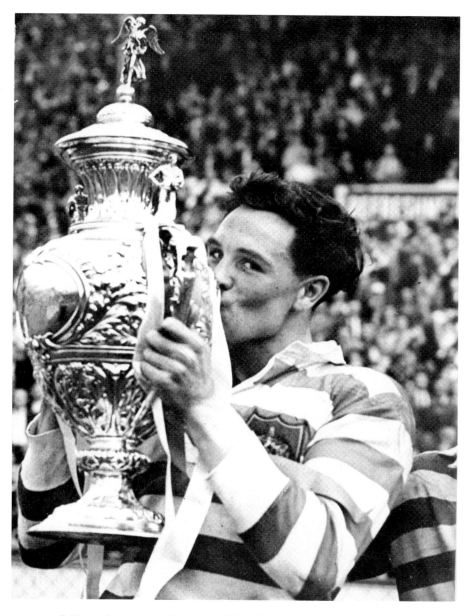

Getting to know you ... Once more Wigan Captain, Eric Ashton, leads his side
to victory in the Rugby League Challenge Cup Final at Wembley

N.B. All photo captions are as per original book

Left: One that didn't get away. Wigan's Eric Ashton is held firmly by a Workington player as another burly team-mate comes up to make doubly sure.

Above: It's August, 1955, and twenty-year-old Eric Ashton is playing in his first match for Wigan's senior team ... and on his way to scoring his first try.

Left: It's all go, go, go ... when you've just snapped up a Billy Boston pass (grounded, on left) ... and your name is Eric Ashton ... and you've just left that former Leeds maestro Lewis Jones clutching at thin air.

Above: Elusive as a shadow. That was Eric Ashton in one of his many moments of glory when he toured Australia in 1958.

Above: 'There's no escape, lad!' is written all over Ashton's face as he flies in to tackle an Australian player at Sydney Cricket Ground.

Above: A trio of heroes in a practice stint at famed Surfer's Paradise in Great Britain's Ashes-winning tour of Australia in 1958. From the left: courageous, big-shouldered, big-hearted Alan Prescott, Eric Ashton and Vince Karalius, flinging out one of his typical right-to-the-target passes

Above: Eric Ashton, as hundreds of opposing players have seen him. Only this time he's in swimming trunks, and running alongside him on that Australian beach is his Great Britain Rugby League team-mate, Gerry Round (Wakefield Trinity).

Left: A spot of fun on the tough 1958 British Rugby League team's tour of Australia and New Zealand ... Skipper Alan Prescott gets a rub-down after a swim from (*left to right*) Alex Murphy, Mick Sullivan and Eric Ashton.

Below: No help needed from big Brian Edgar, that fine Workington forward, as Eric Ashton grounds a Kiwi when Great Britain pile on the pressure in a match in New Zealand.

Above: Australia's Ian Walsh escapes the clutches of a fallen Great Britain player in this fine action shot during the Second Test at Brisbane in 1962. British Rugby League players are (*from left*): Brian McTigue, Brian Edgar, Bill Sayer and Eric Ashton, wearing his captaincy no. 1 jersey. Aussie players (*left to right*) are: Gasnier, Beattie, Carson, Vivers and Banks.

Eric Ashton's Hall of fame: (*Top left*) Mighty Mac ... And it's Brian McTigue in action. (*Top right*) One that got away! And it's Billy Boston eluding a Hull player as he sets off on a typical block-busting run. (*Bottom left*) Caught! Or is he? A fine action shot of spring-heeled Alex Murphy, of St. Helens and Great Britain fame.
(*Bottom right*) Australian Reg Gasnier, one of the best-ever Rugby League centre three-quarters, is a model of class and efficiency as he demonstrates how to accept a pass.

Above: Fitness ... fitness ... fitness.   Ask any of these four international Rugby League backs ... Alan Davies, Eric Ashton, Mick Sullivan and Glyn Moses ...   and they will agree it's essential during an arduous Australian tour.   Watching his 'boys' training at Sydney Cricket Ground is shirt-sleeved team manager, Tom Mitchell.

Below: Even New South Wales captain Tony Paskins throws a 'Well done, boy!' look at victorious Great Britain skipper, Eric Ashton, as they lead their depleted team off their battlefield 'Down Under' in May, 1962.   Six players - including Great Britain's Billy Boston, Mick Sullivan and Bill Sayer - were sent off in this turbulent clash with New South Wales.

job well, exceptionally well, and get out of the way of trouble at the same time.

'I put him in the Billy Boston class. Different playing style, of course. But just as good to see when "The Van" is in full flight and streaking down his wing for his opponents' line.'

Ice-cool Phil Jackson, of Barrow, won hands down that 'shadow team' place in the centre. He must be on anybody's list of the top post-war centres. A natural footballer, with the strength and style of the ideal inside back, he made two successful tours of Australia. Some of his tries had to be seen to be believed, and his proudest moment came when he captained Great Britain in July, 1958, in the third Ashes-winning Test.

Captain of the French World Cup side in 1957, Merquey was a little on the small side. But believe me, he was a real mighty atom. Tricky, fast and elusive ... and excellent handler of a ball ... and a fair opponent.

Brian Bevan, Ray Price and Australia's Holman are automatic choices. I cannot add anything to the hundreds of thousands of words that have already been written about 'Bev', the bald-headed touch-down ace. He has scored more tries - more than 800 of them - than any other Rugby League or Rugby Union player anywhere.

Bevan signed for Warrington in 1946, and hit his peak in the following seasons:

1947-48	...	...	...	57 tries
1948-49	...	...	...	56 tries
1950-51	...	...	...	68 tries
1951-52	...	...	...	51 tries
1952-53	...	...	...	72 tries
1953-54	...	...	...	67 tries
1954-55	...	...	...	63 tries
1955-56	...	...	...	53 tries
1957-58	...	...	...	46 tries
1958-59	...	...	...	54 tries

Glory In The Centre Spot

Brilliant Bevan, who helped Warrington to win all the major trophies, and pulled in the crowds like some powerful magnet on every club ground in Lancashire, Yorkshire and Cumberland, had a 'lean spell' in the twilight of his career at Wilderspool Stadium.

'Bev' only scored ninety tries in his last three seasons with Warrington. Most clubs would be darned thankful if they had a three-quarter on their books who could average thirty tries a season.

Alan Prescott goes in at No. 8 in the front row of the forwards - an obvious choice - and Australian Brian Davies, who could play open-side or blind-side prop positions with equal ease, goes in at No. 10.

I have played so long with ex-Wigan team-mate Bill Sayer, and admired his skill for season after season, that he must edge out every other hooker in the business ... except, naturally, Ian Walsh, who strolled into my world team.

Dick Huddart, now going like a bomb in Australian Rugby League, was an automatic choice for our international side since his devastating first appearance in the Great Britain side in Australia in 1958. No use adding anything to the record of a tremendous player which simply speaks for itself.

Derek ('Rocky') Turner in the second row? And why not? He is far too good to leave out. For Turner always played a 'blinder' whether it was at loose-forward, in the middle row, or propping, as he did towards the end of his remarkable career with Wakefield in the 1965-66 season.

A terrific player both in the loose and in a tight corner ... and ideal tourist international when the chips are down ... a forward and captain in the Valentine, Whiteley, Karalius mould.

Johnny Raper, of New South Wales, is the last man to pack down in my second-choice 'big-six'. He first toured over here in 1959, and ranks among Australia's truly great loose-forwards. He had some rare tussles with New

Zealand's Mel Cooke, and England's Whiteley, Turner and Karalius.

Clever in attack, Raper is an exceptionally fine tackler in close work, and his cover is similarly effective. Indeed, Raper has been one of the most mobile men I have ever met for a loose-forward.

Well, those are my teams. No doubt, there are one or two surprise choices in certain positions. To me, there is only one intriguing thought: Which side would have come out on top if they had ever met?

Glory In The Centre Spot

9

ROOM FOR IMPROVEMENT

This game of mine ranks among the most gripping spectacles you will find anywhere in the sporting calendar. I will argue that with anybody. It can crackle with thrills and skill. It is the truest test I know of a man's toughness and determination.

Which makes all the sadder the inescapable and unpleasant fact that Rugby League is slowly, remorselessly, committing suicide. That's right ... SUICIDE.

Because, after ten years in its top tanks, I am more than ever convinced that only drastic re-thinking by the men who rule the game will heal up the self-inflicted wounds that are killing it.

There is just one word I would like to keep on ramming into these elder statesmen. That word is *progress*. It is the opposite of standing still. And that is exactly what Rugby League has been doing far too obviously for far too long.

Standing still on the vital issue of pay: the one inducement that would reopen the rapidly closing pipeline of fresh young talent we just cannot do without.

Standing still when it comes to insisting on strength of character and firmness - plain, no-nonsense toughness - among referees.

Standing still instead of trying to broaden the whole outlook of the game by making it an attractive, all-week-long social set-up instead of just a Saturday afternoon match and nothing else.

It is about time someone did some plain talking on all three, because only plain talk and positive action are going to stop Rugby League from drifting into oblivion in a few years' time.

Maybe the old ideas were good enough fifteen and twenty years ago. Maybe the 'take it or leave it' attitude was fine when entertainment was scarce, and watching a Saturday afternoon thriller was the pinnacle of the week.

The trouble is, times have changed a lot since then. But Rugby League hasn't. And the wise men of Chapeltown Road, Leeds, the throne-room of the game, had better start accepting that fact.

Let's take a look at the side of the crisis that is closest to the players themselves. That, of course, is PAY. The reward for two nights given up every week for training and eighty minutes of all-out effort - with a strong risk of injury - on a Saturday.

There is nothing more calculated to bring a sharp and sardonic crack from the hard-bitten men of Rugby League than talk of some soccer *prima donna* asking for the earth. And usually getting it.

Can you blame us? We train hard. And the game we play takes a lot of topping for sheer ruggedness and physical danger. Yet what is the carrot they hold out to tempt a promising youngster into a world like that, and ask him to get his head knocked off?

I'll tell you. The 'A' team pay for a win is £5. For getting beaten the pay packet is a bulging £3. Hardly the crock of gold, is it? Hardly enough to make a lad give up his weekend overtime in a nice, safe job, to plough through the mud-and-blood apprenticeship that Rugby League demands.

And when he makes it? When he reaches the big time, what can he expect? My club, Wigan, is probably the biggest of the big time. By Rugby League standards their terms are generous. The basic winning pay is £12.

In fairness to Wigan, I will say that I have never had to draw the basic pay. It has always been more. But clubs like mine are rarities. Only a select few, like St Helens, Wakefield, Leeds and Swinton will offer terms to match that.

In some cases a player's winning pay is no more than £9 or £10. Not so long ago losing money was raised to £7 a match. Not so much, is it, when you realise that in 1939 the figure was £5.

Of course, the argument the Rugby League bosses throw at you is the old one: 'We don't pay you to get beaten.'

All very well. Good, hard-headed Northern logic. Except that it doesn't hold too much water. You can often pour as much effort into a game that is lost as you can into a victory.

When we compare ourselves to the highly-paid soccer stars, we are told that there isn't really any comparison because for them sport is a full-time job, while we are part-timers.

What they don't say is that a soccer man goes on drawing his money when he is out of action after being injured in the service of his club. All we are given when we break and dislocate our bones is the princely sum of £4 Rugby League insurance money a week.

Can you wonder that there is growing disillusionment among the players? They are professionals. They feel their skills demand a fair price.

But the real danger, as I have said, is the effect that this cheese-paring is having on the boys who have the natural ability and the will to succeed. What they don't have is the inclination to submit to a rigorous training schedule twice a week so that they can get battered around at the end of it - with just peanuts to show in their pay packets.

It is very difficult to find fault with their reasoning on that score ...

Now, the men who can make or break a match just as easily as the players themselves. I'm talking about the referees.

Perhaps it seems strange that a player, a captain and a coach should be complaining that referees are too lenient. After all, the 'softer' they are the more you are going to get away with. And every escape raises your chances of winning.

Well, I'm sorry, but I don't go along with that at all. As far as I am concerned an easy-going or timid referee is a positive menace. He does the game a whole lot of harm.

The trouble is, there are far too many referees today who slot into those categories. Men who let themselves be exploited far too easily.

There are only four men I can bring to my mind who command my full respect as referees, which is a pretty sad commentary after watching referees in action for as long as I have.

You know, when they are in the middle, that you have to watch out or you are likely to be heading for an early shower. They are in among you all the time, sorting you out, ticking you off. Making you toe their line. Which is exactly as it should be.

What a glaring pity it is that there should be only four of that calibre - and others who could appear to be literally men of straw, bending with the will of the crowd, swayed and possibly intimidated by the players.

I have lost count of the number of times I have seen a player get as many as four warnings for lying offside, and still be around at the final whistle.

What good is that? What is the point of being backed up by a rule book and virtually tossing it away?

Of course, the bleat from some referees is that the club coaches are to blame. They complain that coaches instruct their men to play offside to smother the opposition.

Naturally, coaches do exactly that if it is going to help them to win. But if they knew the referee was going to crack down hard every time it happened, I'm pretty sure they would soon stop it.

No, that excuse just won't do. A referee is put there, and paid, to control a game. To make sure it is run according to the rules. When he fails to do that - and the failure rate is getting far too high now - the result is a mess that reflects no credit at all on Rugby League.

One way to make sure that referees handled their jobs efficiently would be to put them on a winning and losing pay basis, just like the players.

It shouldn't be beyond Rugby League's rulers to arrange a system of independent observers to watch a referee in action, and decide the payment he merits.

Nobody would be able to complain of bias. Also I am sure that if the referee knew his wallet was going to be affected he would put a lot more thought and effort into HIS game.

But as long as the current inept and unsatisfactory general standard of refereeing is allowed to go on, Rugby League is going to suffer. And, in its present state, the game cannot afford to take too many body blows.

Yes, there is plenty that is wrong with the game on the field. These are problems which must be tackled vigorously for everybody's sake. Most of all, for the sake of the fans.

We ask a lot of them. We ask them to huddle out in the open in all kinds of weather. We ask them to put up with near-primitive conditions on quite a few grounds. We ask them to come and watch too many spoiled games.

The results of policies like that are obvious. Take Wigan, a successful club and the envy of most of the others in the League. Five years ago we were averaging gates of 19,000.

Glory In The Centre Spot

This year the average attendance has dropped to around 8,000.

That is pretty alarming, and among the poorer clubs the position is even more threatening. In too many cases what used to be a flourishing and popular business has become a week-by-week struggle for survival.

The answer to putting Rugby League back on the up-grade could lie, to a large extent, away from the field. It could lie in the build-up of the social side of club life - to make the club something that really belongs to the whole town, whether they are keen on the game or not.

In this respect, Britain is lagging way behind places like Australia. You have only to look at the St George club in Sydney to realise the possibilities there are.

St George get along on gates of about nine thousand, and they play only sixteen league games a year. Yet they can afford to pay their top player £1,600, and no one is on less than £1,000 a year.

Why? The answer is simple. St George think big. Their minds aren't just on the game itself. The game is just the centre-piece of a very big business. They have a seven-storey £2,000,000 club that has to be seen to be believed. Fruit machines clicking all day long; plush restaurants and bars. The lot.

There are St George club ties. There are St George club lighters. All bringing in money. The members meet the players on a free and easy footing. They aren't just remote figures in jerseys. They are the people eating dinner with *you*.

Compare luxury like that with what the average English Rugby League fan has to put up with on his Saturday afternoon out. Afternoon out! We make it just about as attractive as a visit to the dentist.

He can have a meat pie, all right. Or tea in a plastic cup. If he is lucky there is a bar - and pretty basic affairs most of them are, too. People crammed shoulder to shoulder, beer spilling everywhere. A whole atmosphere of seediness.

The miracle is that so many fans are still prepared to come along and endure it. They deserve something better, and the change would only bring the benefit of more money to the clubs themselves.

The small-time attitude that grips the game here starts right at the top. When Australia's Rugby League bosses meet, it is in a great palace of a place, well laced with restaurants and bars.

Our game is ruled from that shabby building in Chapeltown Road at Leeds. The council members have to nip down the road to a restaurant if they want a meal. The facilities are absolutely nil.

A small point? Perhaps it is, but that is the real trouble. Rugby League in England is full of too many small points like this.

There is talk of trying to expand the game - trying to popularise it in other parts of the country. The point, surely, is that if we are going to keep it popular in the North alone we are going to have to think bigger, act bigger, and get right down to some sweeping changes.

The alternative - and I will say it again - is the death of a great game!

Glory In The Centre Spot

10

'GLORY IN THE CENTRE SPOT'

I stand 6 ft. 1 in. tall in my stockinged feet. I tip the scales at about 14 stone 4 lbs. There were times in Australia, however, when I wished I had been twice as tall - and almost twice as heavy.

Admittedly, the occasions were only few. But they were there all the same. Moments when your strength and football ability don't seem sufficient ... moments when only your heart, beating faster than normal under that Great Britain jersey, is carrying you through against opposition of the most fierce, tigerish quality.

Guts. Sheer guts. You name it. We had to have it on every trip - and there have been three of them - that I made to Australia.

I have toured 'Down Under' with men of immense courage. Like Alan Prescott. I have toured with a player who whipped up a hate complex against the Aussies before any important game. Like Vince Karalius. I have toured with a player who hardly once played to his true form.

There is no room for sentimentality out there in

Australia. There are twenty-six players in a Rugby League Test tour party - twenty-six working lads from clubs in Lancashire, Yorkshire and Cumberland. A bunch of hard grafters, living out of suitcases, who soon become the closest-knit community on God's earth.

You are playing in the toughest game in the world. And, whether it be Sydney or Brisbane, you are smack in the enemy's camp. The climate, the tension, and the ruggedness of the play are all different from that at Wakefield and Warrington, Wigan and Workington, Barrow and Bramley, Huddersfield and Hunslet. Certainly you have the feeling it is all so different. And certainly it knots your stomach ... makes you, at times, play above yourself ... and forces you, always, to go into the tackle that little bit harder.

No, there are no beg-pardons in Rugby League football in Australia. You don't get them. You don't expect them. For you are only too well aware that you are up against Rugby players who are bitter when they lose. Men who want to win right from the word 'go' - and don't give a tuppenny damn who knows it.

We always seem to support the underdogs. Not the Kangaroos of Rugby League. Those Aussies are only for Australia. I don't condemn them for it. In fact, I applaud it.

There's no half-heartedness about their efforts. Some say they are show-offs. Tommy-rot! The Aussies simply like to be top-dogs. Their attitude is the right one. They give you some 'stick' out there in big matches in more ways than one. Even beer cans, oranges and apple cores, in incidents I will describe later, have been tossed on to pitches by irate, jeering fans.

Before I tell you my own story about some of the games in Australasia, which I will always remember vividly, I would like to emphasise again that in order to succeed in this great game of Rugby League there must be no room for sentiment for the second-best.

On the contrary, if you can beat them by a clear sixty

points then do just that. Harsh? Maybe. But it's the cold truth. For, as I have hinted already, most of Britain's sport would benefit if we took a leaf out of that Australian notebook. Certainly there is an outsize chance there would be an improvement in the results - in our favour.

Now let me turn to my baptism in tour football - that '57 World Cup series in Australia. It is history now that of the countries taking part, the others being France, New Zealand and Australia, the Great Britain side finished last.

Although, as they say in Lancashire and Yorkshire, we 'broke no pots' in Australia, at least one thing emerged: I had landed on my feet as a Great Britain player of the future. It makes me blush now when I glance back through my early scrapbook and see those newspaper headlines ...

'Eric Ashton Star of World Cup Tour'
'Ashton Stars in Rugby League Defeat'
'Ashton Booked As A Star of The Future'
'Ashton Try Trio Steals The Show'

Well, even if our touring side's hopes had been dashed, my own lucky star seemed to be zooming. All the more surprising really when I remember only making the trip as a late selection.

Up to then, the furthest that I had ever travelled from my home at St Helens was by boat to the Isle of Man! Honestly, I never expected to be included in the party of eighteen players chosen to represent England in the World Cup.

When the selectors met they picked a team to meet France at St Helens. That was the front-line side which would also make the World Cup trip. Then they added five dual-position men: Hooker Tom McKinney (St Helens), centre Alan Davies (Oldham), loose-forward Johnny Whiteley (Hull), half-back Austin Rhodes (St Helens), and myself. And, like young Rhodes, I was stepping up to top stardom for the fist time.

111

Alan Prescott, the big Saints front-row man, was our captain, thus adding yet another honour to this twelve-month list:

Led St Helens to their first Wembley Cup win;

Carried off the Lance Todd Trophy as the best player in the Wembley final;

Voted the Player of the Year;

Led Lancashire to victory in the county championships;

Captained Great Britain to victory in the Test matches against Australia.

I thought I hadn't got a hope of going 'Down Under'. I reckoned there were a lot of others in front of me. Yet I was the surprise centre selection - and there were few quibbles with the team as a whole.

I thoroughly enjoyed the trip. I played in ten of the twelve matches in Australia and South Africa, where we were 'showing the flag' in three exhibition matches with the Frenchmen. In all, I notched fifteen tries and kicked five goals.

In some games we went like a bomb. In some of the important ones - which clinched the series for the Aussies - we seemed to fumble, falter and fritter away chances.

We soon found brilliant form in torrential rain in Brisbane and then, hampered by injuries and a sudden lapse of form by certain players, lost it in vital matches.

I'll not forget that Brisbane tussle in a hurry. We thrashed Queensland, who were fielding six current internationals, by 44 points to 5. And they don't come much better than that.

We were credited with a storming display of precision handling. I scored a hat-trick of tries between the 14th and 20th minutes. Mick Sullivan got four tries. Additional tries came from Prescott, Whiteley, Rhodes, Geoff Gunney and Derek Turner. Rhodes and Lewis Jones landed two goals each.

I was having the sort of debut any kid dreams about. Less than a year earlier I had embarked on my Rugby League career at Wigan. And here I was, trying to throw my weight about among the elite of the Rugby League world. Let's face it, a bit of luck must have been on my side, too. For most things I tried to pull off worked like a dream. Moreover, to the Aussies I was something of a 'dark horse'. I was soon getting good write-ups in their Press, however, and was happy to be justifying my selection for the tour.

My market value to Wigan must have rocketed following my performances on the left wing and at centre. Ironically, in my two appearances for Great Britain against other countries, and also when I played for 'The Rest', I only came into the team on each occasion because of injuries.

That personal success in Australia atoned in some way for the keen disappointment I had felt a few months earlier, when I had failed with a vital goal-kick in a cup-tie against Leeds.

One Rugby League writer put it this way: 'Oddly enough, Ashton and Whiteley, two British reserves, are the only ones to have emerged from the World Cup visit with any great credit, apart from Phil Jackson. Yet Ashton never considered himself worthy of selection for the World Cup, and scoffed at my prediction that he would be selected.'

I thoroughly enjoyed my rugby in the World Cup final. I started on the left wing for 'The Rest' against champions Australia, who incidentally beat us by 20 points to 11. I moved to centre when Gilbert Benausse had been out of action with a stiff-armed tackle three minutes after half-time.

Benausse was hit by a late tackle from Hawick and was found to be suffering from concussion. I managed to make ground in possession and went over for a try late in the proceedings. We gave some bright entertainment to the crowd of 30,000 which was above expectations, and for the Australians Carlson gave an outstanding display at full-back, his tackling saving four certain tries.

It was later, playing for a combined Great Britain and France Northern Hemisphere side against New Zealand, at Carlaw Park, that I hit the jackpot. For our combined English and French team finished ahead by 34 points to 31 ... *and I scored five tries and kicked five goals.* A personal tally of twenty-five points in one match. It established a new record in internationals. The highest previous tally had come from Lewis Jones (Leeds) against France, when he scored a total of 23 points.

A newspaper report of the match said: 'This was Wigan centre Eric Ashton's day. He moved well on the muddy ground, scoring five tries and landing five goals.

'The combined side were reduced to eleven men half-way through the second half, because of injuries to the Frenchmen Levy and Appelian, but they still managed to hold a rejuvenated Kiwi attack.

'The combined side led 19-2 at half-time after some lack-lustre play the by New Zealanders.

'Ashton was easily the outstanding player on the field. After him came the ginger-haired captain, Alan Prescott.

'Prescott showed grand leadership, pounding the Kiwis into the mud with some fine tackling, and more often than not figured in the tries.

'The combined side battled along with only four forwards to Kiwis' five, Maori prop Maxwell also having been injured.

'Among the other British players, the most impressive were the nippy Leeds half-back, Jeff Stevenson, and loose-forward Turner, who moved to stand-off after Levy's injury.

'Levy lost skin and hair in a head injury and Appelian was taken off on a stretcher to have six stitches inserted in a gash on the forehead.

'A crowd of 15,000 saw some disappointing play from the home team, who never looked like an international side until after the interval. Then they got much more of the ball and made good use of it.'

Concerning those homeward-bound exhibition games in South Africa, in which our Great Britain boys played the French. I don't think they were of much value, although we did enjoy ourselves. I doubt if Rugby League will ever go big in South Africa. My impression was that their spectators, while knowledgeable about the amateur Union code, hadn't a clue about the Rugby League rule-book.

In fact, they simply laughed at some of the things we did on the field. For instance, when they saw a burly forward bend down and play the ball between his legs. They'd been brought up on Union. For the vast majority, this was their first glimpse at Rugby League. Also, unfortunately, each of the three exhibition games was played before a different crowd and the same reaction arose on each occasion. Only when a match was about two-thirds over were spectators beginning to get the hang of things.

I did learn one thing in South Africa which absolutely staggered me. That is, if I had been a player in South Africa's purely amateur Rugby Union code, I would have been found a plum £60-a-week job to prevent me joining the paid ranks! Seemed funny at the time. Especially when the official programme for our exhibition games in South Africa listed me as a labourer! Which, of course, was perfectly true in those days in my hometown, St Helens.

It was in the following year, 1958, that I was given my first opportunity to captain a Rugby League Test touring team. Again, I was back in Australia, the second time inside twelve months that I was spending my summer holidays on the beaches of Sydney and Brisbane, and on the playing pitches of Australia's famous rugby and cricket grounds.

Lucky for some. Lucky for Eric Ashton. For, as always, following our struggle for the Ashes in Australia, the Great Britain R.L. party always moves across to New Zealand for a two-test series. And it was at Auckland on August 12th - a truly 'Glorious Twelfth' - that I first led out our international side in a Test match.

Firstly, however, I mustn't let this opportunity slip by without relating what had happened in the three Tests against the Kangaroos.

The Lions' tail was really twisted before a record Test

crowd of 67,637 at Sydney, when Great Britain lost the first of the three-match series by 25 points to 8.

This was the Great Britain line-up: E. Fraser (Warrington); I. Southward (Workington), P. Jackson (Barrow), A. Davies (Oldham), M. Sullivan (Wigan); D. Bolton (Wigan), A. Murphy (St Helens); A. Terry (St Helens), T. Harris (Hull), A. Prescott (St Helens), M. Martyn (Leigh), B. Edgar (Workington), J. Whiteley (Hull).

Our lads were crushed by five goals and five tries to one goal and two tries. They were trailing by thirteen clear points after only fifteen minutes' play. There had been omissions, which proved to be fatal, of forwards Dick Huddart and Brian McTigue from our team. There was no Vince Karalius around, since he had been suspended following an incident in our rough-house against New South Wales. Finally, there had been referee Darcy Lawler's pre-match warning: 'I'll have clean play ... or else.'

Our boys took him at his word. Result: They were floored right from the start. Centre Davies was whizzed off his feet, put out of action for a short period, and was little more than a passenger afterwards. Half-back Bolton was knocked out with a crack in the face and had to be carried off. All this, plus little fire in Great Britain's play, added up the Kangaroo's clear-cut win.

At Brisbane we levelled the series one-all by a 25-18 win. And what a win! And at what a cost! Five players were taken to hospital.

This had been the match Great Britain had to win at all costs. They did it by a superhuman effort in a sizzling, cruel game which turned out to be a touring side's finest hour in Rugby League history since that 'Battle of Rorke's Drift', when a British R.L. side won with only ten men on the field at the finish.

There were two moments of high drama. The first came on the field when Alan Prescott's forearm was broken in the first minutes. After the fourth scrum hooker Tommy Harris told Prescott: 'These scrums are getting a bit loose, skipper.' Prescott replied: 'Sorry, Tom, my arm is broken. We'll say nowt about it now, though.'

The second moment came off the field in the Great Britain dressing-room at half-time, when the Lions were leading 10-2. Bolton was out of the game. Challinor and Karalius were injured. 'Precky' was holding that broken arm. Team manager Tom Mitchell said to Prescott: 'It's up to you, Alan.' And 'Precky' replied: 'I'll carry on, Tom.' He even refused a pain-killing injection from a doctor. And he led the lads - just twelve of them - out into that blazing sun. It was one of the finest displays of courage I've ever seen. 'Precky' never once complained. He and Karalius whipped the injury-hit team into a relentless, blood-and-guts force that tanned the pants of those Kangaroos in sensational style.

In the third and deciding 1958 Test at Sydney before a 'gate' of 68,720 the Australians were well and truly whipped by 40 points to 17.

Twenty minutes before the end a big section of the crowd were hurling orange peel, rubbish, bottles and beer cans on to the field. Now I feel those spectators were pelting that stuff at their own players - not at our team, not at referee Jack Casey. They felt that Ian Moir, Keith Holman, Norman Provan and Company - their heroes until this moment of truth - had let them down badly. Hence the barrage. It was Karalius who grinned at Mick Sullivan (three tries) and said: 'I wish they'd throw us some proper fruit, Sully ... I could murder two or three oranges right now.'

So on to New Zealand. Phil Jackson, as he had been in that third and deciding Test in Australia, was again captain in the absence of Prescott. We were a big disappointment, losing by 15 points to 10. For our second and final Test my old team-mate and pal, Jackson, was dropped.

Phil took it very well. He knew, as we all did, that his form, for some unknown reason, was well below that of the real, classy Jackson.

117

I had been skipper on occasions in the 'country' games. But this was my baptism as leader of a Great Britain Rugby League Test side. Tom Mitchell, who had done a grand job on this tour with his co-manager, 'Barney' Manson, told me: 'We've decided to appoint you captain. We think you're the best man for the job. It's the chance of a life-time. Grab it with both hands.'

I did just that. We won by 32 points to 15. And this was our team: Fraser (Warrington); Southward (Workington), Ashton (Wigan), Challinor (Warrington), Sullivan (Wigan); Davies (Oldham), Murphy (St Helens), Edgar (Workington), Harris (Hull), McTigue (Wigan), Goodwin (Barrow), Huddart (Whitehaven), Karalius (St Helens).

I ran in a couple of tries. Yet Mick Sullivan, who had a storming game, went one better. Murphy grabbed his customary try. Eric Fraser added the points to all six tries, besides landing a penalty.

It was the 1962 tour of Australia - a record-breaking affair in more ways than one - that I fully understood the full responsibilities of a fully-fledged, firmly-established Great Britain touring side skipper.

I worked it out this way; If I was going to do a captain's job on tour according to the book, then I was going to be a very lonely man.

All Rugby League touring team skippers do get one preference over the rest. There's not a scrap of difference in their pay packets. But they can have a room of their own at all hotels on this lengthy trip. I turned down the offer. I simply said I wanted to room-mate, as I always had done previously, with my old pal Alex Murphy. And that's what I did.

I got a good name on that tour. I even got the rating as the best skipper of any Great Britain R.L. tour party. Well, much of the credit for that is due to the players who made my task such an easy one at times.

We were a well-balanced, fine, successful side. The lads

were well-behaved off the field. There were no trouble-makers. It has become pretty common among some Rugby Union tour teams to 'smash-up' a hotel or two in after-the-match celebrations. None of that from the working lads who were with me and playing their hearts out on our '62 tour. I had to issue remarkably few 'do's' and 'don't's' ... there were no moans from any of them ... no skipper could have asked for more.

Furthermore, when it came to choosing the actual Test line-ups I made sure there were no shocks or glum faces from any of the boys. You find you have some 'ham-and-eggers' in every football tour party - players who aren't quite up to the standard of your speedily-assessed first-choice thirteen. You soon spot your No. 1 thirteen from the 26 who have made the trip. So I decided not to shove up my Test team on a hotel noticeboard without first having a quiet word with a few of those who hadn't made the grade on that particular occasion. I reasoned that by doing this, the announcement of the team wouldn't come as a surprise.

Also, by doing this I was cutting complaints to a minimum. A splendid example of the excellent team-spirit of that 1962 tour party came from Laurie Gilfedder, who was then at Warrington and is now on Wigan's books. 'Gilly' played in most of our games in Australia, yet he only caught our side in one Test match. And that was only because regular loose-forward Derek ('Rocky') Turner had to cry-off the second Test at Brisbane. Not a single moan or groan from Gilfedder, a top-class sportsman on and off the field.

I soon discovered that the secret of handling, coaxing and soothing players was TACT. It's the way that you actually say things to them that counts. Cut out the bullying unless it is absolutely necessary in a situation. Don't be aloof. Just because you're captain it doesn't make you one scrap different from any of them. And, at all times, treat them like MEN ... men who are pulling their guts out for you and their Rugby League fans back home. Men who will understand when you have to be iron-handed at times on the field. Men who will appreciate it if you never try to treat them like a bunch of kids. Get to understand them quickly, gain their confidence about everything, and the battle is already half-won.

Well, the Ashton plan of treating 'em right seemed to work out in that Australian sunshine in '62. We came within a cat's whisker - a single point, to be precise - of becoming the first-ever British Rugby League side to win all three Tests in Australia.

The first, at Sydney, we won by 31 points to 12. In the second, at Brisbane, we clinched it with a 17-10 victory. And back at Sydney, for the third and final Test, we were beaten by 18 points to 17.

The Aussies dithered and dallied when we completely outplayed them in the opening Test match in Sydney. The attendance was 69,000 (receipts, £29,582). To be blunt about it, we were humiliating them before the end.

The big guns of Gasnier, Irvine and Cleary were all spiked - despite the fact that the Kangaroos had been leading by 7 points to nil after only five minutes' play.

British players like Turner, McTigue and 'Tiger' Huddart (despite being in a daze for half an hour) were in their element. They did a magnificent carving-up job of the big Australian forwards. For once, Alex Murphy, the boy for the big occasion, had a quiet game. On the other hand, Boston, Sullivan, Fox and Bolton were on brilliant form.

Again, angry Australian fans pelted apples on the Sydney Cricket Ground as we knocked the stuffing out of their team. Our try-scorers were: Sullivan (two), Ashton (two), Turner, Huddart, Boston. And five goals were banged through the Aussie sticks by Wakefield Trinity's Neil Fox.

At Brisbane, on June 30, 1962, it was the first time since 1928 that a British touring side had won the first two Tests. It was also my proudest moment as an international skipper. We had held the Ashes. The Aussies had taken a hammering. And for Billy Boston it was an afternoon of sheer triumph. Bouncing Billy grabbed two tries - and the Australians' plan to knock him off his game with two-and three-men tackles went completely hay-wire. Our other try before a 32,000 'gate' (receipts £19,000) came from mercurial Murphy. Fox kicked three goals and I managed to drop a goal.

Finally, the third Test at Sydney. We were winning by 17 points to 13 with only seconds to go. A try in the corner and the Aussies were breathing down our necks. Ken Irvine - not a recognised goal-kicker - landed a fine goal from the touchline. And the Australians had scraped home with a narrow win - their consolation prize of the series.

I have said that the second Test match at Brisbane was my best moment as Great Britain skipper. My worst? Just for the record, it was over here against the New Zealanders in 1961.

We had gone into an 8-2 lead in the first Test at Leeds. Everything seemed to be plain sailing ... and then everything went wrong.

We lost by 26 points to 13. Of course, heads had to roll. Mine was one of them.

Now, on this particular occasion, I don't honestly think I deserved to be axed. We had lost. And we had made a mess of it. Yet I didn't consider I had done all that badly. I *know* when I haven't been up to scratch. I have been around on the international Rugby League scene too long to need people to tell me when I've had an off-day. It wasn't all that much of an off-day for Ashton at Leeds. But some folk begged to differ ... and I was dropped.

Nothing new, really. I had been dropped before - and managed to come back. Luckily, I managed to do just that for the 1962 Australasian Tour ... a tour of warm memories, bitterly-fought battles, and firm friendships ... a tour which made me proud to be wearing the jersey of a *great* Great Britain Rugby League side's skipper.

121

Glory In The Centre Spot

11

PUTTING YOU IN THE PICTURE

The name is firmly planted for all-time in Rugby League's hall of fame: Jim Sullivan. It ranks with Jack Dempsey in boxing; Sir Stanley Matthews in soccer; and Sir Gordon Richards in racing.

Big Jim, the hard man from Wales who made the biggest stars around jump smartly when he cracked the whip. And that was often. Big Jim, one of the greatest coaches of them all.

I am not going to dispute his claim to being just that. Here I am simply using Sullivan as an example of the myth I want to explode about the coaching business. The myth that a coach can work wonders. That the best coaches are miracle men.

Take a look at what happened with Sullivan. He built his reputation with a Wigan team that was surely the most talent-packed of the post-war era. He carried it on with St Helens. Again, top talent was there waiting to be exploited. And, with Sullivan at the helm, Saints zoomed upwards.

But what happened when the vaunted Sullivan moved

on to Rochdale, strong on toughness, but palpably short on simple, natural, in-born skill?

The answer is right there in the record books for anyone to examine. The humble Hornets didn't move one inch up in the League or one yard nearer to Wembley. They remained exactly what they had been, even with the magnificent Sullivan at the controls. They were, let's face it, uninspired mediocrities.

Today it has become the practice, when a team is doing well, to give an even bigger share of the credit to the coach than to the players. The fans talk lovingly and glowingly of the man behind the scenes. The man who has made it all possible.

What a load of eye-wash! Of course, a good coach will guide a team on the right lines, map out its tactics. If he has the talent there in the first place. Because, if it isn't there, it is impossible to create.

And Sullivan proved precisely that point ...

Examine the teams that are, pretty well, Rugby League's constant attractions. Teams like Widnes, Warrington, St Helens, Wakefield ...

True, they all have coaches who rank as the tops. Joe Egan, Ernie Ashcroft, Joe Coan, Ken Traill. But I am sure every one of these four will agree with me. What has kept them up there, more than their own skills, has been the steady supply of good local talent.

Don't get me wrong. I am not knocking the valuable role that the coaches play in the game. The good ones can inspire fine players to be even better. But, in the end, the player has got to have it in himself if he is going to make the grade. No coach in the world can put it there.

What, then, is the real function of a coach, apart from instilling confidence, having the ability to read and plan a game, and having the strength of character to control a team of highly-strung professionals?

So far as I am concerned at Wigan, it boils down to this:

Turning out a side that is as fit as it is possible for thirteen men to be. Because even brilliance can go horribly wrong when peak fitness is not there to sustain it right through a gruelling game.

And when you are dealing with men as hard-bitten and battle-hardened as top Rugby League players, that can be quite a job. Because I do not believe any one of them can honestly say he enjoys the sheer physical grind of training two nights a week.

I will be honest myself. I have always hated that side of the business. My old pal Billy Boston would be the first to admit the same thing.

It is so easy, when you know you have the ability that is needed, to start thinking: 'I'll skip it tonight. I'll get by.'

The mistake is a fatal one, yet I know any number of first-class players who will try to pull a fast one on the coach just to get out of the hard labour.

The answer is to make the training stint as attractive as possible. I do not blame anyone for not wanting to do endless push-ups, or haul hulking great weights around, or scamper up and down terrace steps.

I believe good results are possible without too much of that. They are made possible by the simple production of a ball. A rugby ball or even a soccer ball. Give your side a ball to work with, keep them moving with it, and suddenly it isn't like training any more. It's fun, but at the same time they are doing what is necessary to sweat themselves into trim.

You would be surprised at the number of coaches who ignore this simple philosophy. They insist all the time on the heavy stuff, with the result that training becomes a twice-a-week bore. A chore to be dodged whenever possible.

Coaching doesn't end on the training field or in the dressing-room before a match. There is plenty more to it than that. I am talking about the political side of the job. The side that is packed with more headaches than any needle match.

For the coach has to act as the go-between for the players and for the board. The players expect him to listen patiently and sympathetically to the moans and groans they put forward.

At the same time, the board - our employers - expect you to interpret their wishes firmly. Often the two clash. And the coach is right in the middle. There are times, believe me, when I have yearned to be just a simple, straight-forward player again, instead of being expected to be a father confessor and a latter day King Solomon rolled up into one.

But let's get back to skill ... The thing a coach can nurture, coax and watch blossom. *But can never produce.*

When I finally get out of the game, perhaps the most disconcerting thought I will take with me will be the reflection that sheer skill is on a steep decline.

I am not exaggerating when I give you this estimate: Only about one-third of the men playing today possess real, natural talent. The rest are mechanical players, getting by either on old-fashioned toughness or on superior speed.

Take the case - the classic case - of McDonald Bailey, the black flash whose only Rugby League record turned out to be the speed with which he exposed himself as a man without one scrap of hope of ever making the grade.

Arthur Rowe, the Yorkshire blacksmith, was another example. Big, strong and something of a sporting character. He had everything, in fact, except football ability.

There is not a coach in the world who could have done a thing with either Bailey or Rowe. It simply was not there in the first place.

I do not want to be unkind to a more recent convert - Alf Meakin, the high-speed Blackpool winger, and a former member of England's Olympic 'Flying Squad'. But another example of a man who, I believe, will never really make the grade, though I could be proved wrong.

Alf can run with the best of them. He will get some tries by virtue of his speed alone. But the inherent, natural flair for the game is missing. I am never worried when I have to face a simple speed merchant like that.

I know that all he can do is run... more often than not straight into trouble. Alf, and players like him, do not know how to run away from a trap or a tackle.

Again, no coach can put this basic skill into them. They can be improved to a certain degree if they stay around long enough. But only to a certain degree. They will always, in my mind, be 'robot players'. Occasionally shining - but all too easy to hit, stop and crush.

At Wigan I have been lucky. Glamour attracts glamour. If a good boy had the choice of either coming to Wigan, or to a team like Batley, it is obvious which one he is going to choose. And that makes my job all that much easier.

The day that stops happening will be the day the fans stop praising me as a coach. And there will not be one single thing I will be able to do about it.

So you can imagine how sorry I feel for the bulk of coaches in the game. Each week they struggle to produce good results for a board which, in many cases, doesn't understand their problems. They expect miracles - as Rochdale did with Jim Sullivan - and miracles just do not happen in this hard world.

That is why I have only two pieces of advice for any youngster who is thinking of trying his luck in Rugby League.

They are these: If you can pass a ball, you are in with a chance. If you can tackle and move instinctively, likewise, you are in with a chance.

But if you can do neither, and you are hoping that some old player, with the title of coach, is going to teach you how it's done, forget it. Stick to taking your girlfriend for a walk on Saturday afternoons.

You will save yourself an awful lot of headaches and heartaches. And you will save the coach from suffering them, too.

Yes, even a coach at glamour club Wigan!

Glory In The Centre Spot

ORIGINAL APPENDIX (1)

By Jack McNamara
Manchester Evening News Rugby League Writer

Eric Ashton has been one of the great post-war centres. He might not have the classical poise of Ernest Ward or the dash of Australia's Pat Devery, but he has all the basic attributes that make a player a star in this position.

Ashton is a tidy player, rather than a flamboyant one, and he is completely unselfish. He is never a man for the daring risk that could either bring a try or give one away; he is always patient, shrewdly so, and the opportunity he awaits always seems to come.

Ashton gives the impression of complete reliability and the strength of character to treat panic under pressure as an unforgivable weakness. This is what helped to make him such a good captain in Britain's 1962 tour of Australia and New Zealand. The Test disasters in New Zealand might never have happened if Ashton had not had to return home with a leg injury sustained in the last match of the Australian campaign.

Under his captaincy, Britain not only won the 'Ashes', but nearly became the first tourists ever to win a complete Test series in Australia. He had a great side with him, but it takes a good captain to bring out the best in his men. And Ashton did this superbly.

Off the field it was a happy tour, and again the captain must take much of the credit. Ashton had the knack of winning respect by quietness and example; team-mates would never have liked to have let Ashton down. And they would certainly do their darnedest to please him.

Like all great players - the really great ones - Ashton is too busy playing football to be unsporting. He has been a deceptively fast runner and, quite frankly, his gangly build makes him look anything but an international three-quarter. It seems that a proper hefty tackle will snap him in half, and the thought of him stopping any opposing giant in full flight could appear ridiculous.

No man could have belied his appearance more. Few tackles have stopped Ashton and he misses even fewer. Possibly Ashton has been under-appreciated because of his total lack of flashiness. Having watched him play in England, France, Australia and New Zealand, sharp memories of any particular match evade me. Rather, there is an overall picture of an undeviating standard of good performance. If Ashton was a motor car - pardon the comparison! - he would be a Rolls Royce, not a zippy sports car.

On the field he always has a sobering influence on hot-heads - and he has had a few of those to worry about in his time. He is never the sort to question a referee's decision, apart from a polite enquiry, and he makes no more fiery protest at a disputed ruling than a shrug of the shoulders. Not that Ashton is ever the sort of man to be put upon, although he has limitless patience with the *prima donnas* he has had to deal with from time to time. Also, he never believes in on-the-field argument.

Ashton is a genuine thinker about the game, and this is plain from his cool approach to situations on the field and his quick thinking in deciding what best to do. Unlike many players, whose memories never extended much beyond their last match, Ashton can recall teams, dates, results and incidents for most of his playing career.

This must have been a blessing to Arthur Brooks and his colleague, Malcolm Keogh, in helping Eric to compile this book. It is typical of Ashton's thorough approach to Rugby League.

If Ashton had a motto it would surely read: 'Let's get on with the game.' It is the policy he has always preached from Wigan to Wollongong.

Glory In The Centre Spot

ORIGINAL APPENDIX (2)

By Roger Halstead
Oldham Evening Chronicle
Rugby League Correspondent

One of the big complaints with present-day Rugby League football is the shortage of fast, accomplished centres and the tendency of most teams to rely far too much on their heavyweight forwards to engineer the points and the frills.

Eric Ashton, in fact, is one of the last surviving members of a long line of classy inside backs, the type of players who packed in the crowds from Wigan to Woomera ... Not only with the use of brawn, but by the use of sheer, footballing know-how, and their ability to crack defences by one deft pass or one slide-rule kick.

Ice-cool Ashton, Australian tourist, skipper of the club which has always been synonymous with success, and almost as famous in the North as Wigan pier itself, is the type of player any club director would give his right hand to own.

Glory In The Centre Spot

I well remember his first game in the famous cherry and white shirt ... on the wing! He was raw, inexperienced, and obviously regarded by Central Park fans as the weak link in a generally strong footballing chain.

How Ashton has made the fans sit up since those early days!

A player who revels in responsibility, it took him only one season to make the Wigan centre spot his own - and a short time later he was not only a famous fixture in a famous side but skipper as well.

Throughout Rugby League Ashton is respected not only as a player destined for a permanent place in the game's Hall of Fame but a qualified coach, master tactician, and a superb example of the type of personality the present-day game lacks.

I shall never forget a Lancashire Cup second-round game at Oldham last autumn. Wigan were on the receiving end of a trouncing by an Oldham side which swept through to the semi-final with a four-try performance.

But the try of the night was made and scored by the old firm of Ashton and wingman Billy Boston.

Receiving the ball 30 yards out, Ashton was hemmed in by Oldham's quick-covering defence. He hadn't a chance. But the centre put in a pin-point grub kick for Boston to tear up the wing and touch-down.

It was the old master at his best ... and he earned the applause of an appreciative crowd no doubt remembering more glorious years for Wigan - and Eric Ashton.

ORIGINAL APPENDIX (3)

By Joe Humphreys
Daily Mirror Rugby League Writer

The date line: Sunday, August 12, 1958. The place: Auckland, New Zealand.

Bright blue skies...a perfect morning. But for Eric Ashton it was something more than a smashing start to another sunny day. Ahead of him had opened a vast new horizon. The chance to lead Great Britain in Rugby League Test matches both in England and overseas.

For the previous afternoon he had safely launched himself as Britain's captain of the future. But that was only part of the story I had to tell of great triumph which made Britain the undisputed world champions.

There was Eric Fraser, of Warrington, asking to be stood down so that Glyn Moses, his full-back rival from St Helens, could have a last chance of playing in a Test match. Fraser, who had played in the three epic Tests in Australia, felt a little sorry for Glyn.

Glory In The Centre Spot

At the time he told me: 'It's a long way for a player to come and then go back without playing in a single Test.' But perhaps it was as well that Fraser did not get his way.

Before Britain finally crushed the Kiwis by 32 points to 15 in a see-saw of a match they were glad of every one of the seven goals Fraser kicked. They needed Eric Ashton, too.

Twice he jerked Britain back into a game which could - and so nearly did - slip away. In the fourth minute, with his brilliant football skill, Ashton exposed a weakness on the Kiwis' right flank to score.

Then he did a repeat burst to send Mick Sullivan searing away for the first of his three tries. Try as they would, New Zealand could not stop Ashton's gallop.

He made another try for Sullivan which swung the game again in the early seconds of the second half and in the end finished with two tries himself. It was Ashton in top form, setting the pace and playing a real captain's part.

But that was only what Tom Mitchell and Barney Manson, joint managers of the tour, expected of Ashton.

With Alan Prescott, packed off back to Britain with a broken arm, and Phil Jackson, not on his best form, they gave Ashton his chance.

And he just went on the field to prove them so right ...

ORIGINAL APPENDIX (4)

By W. R. Sinclair
of the *Sunday Mirror*

Centre three-quarters in Rugby League can, broadly speaking, be grouped into three categories - the craftsmen, the artists and, small in number but outstanding in the game's history, a small but select band of supremely great exponents.

These are centres who have combined both the foregoing traits and, in addition, possessed that rare ability to dominate a match by sheer force of personality.

Among the latter, however dissimilar in style, could be numbered the legendary Harold Wagstaff, the incomparable Gus Risman, and others of like stature and skill, such as Billy Batten (Hull) and Arthur Atkinson (Castleford). These were giants in every sense of the term. I saw them all and although some, like Batten and Wagstaff, were past their prime, their greatness was still there for all to see.

Glory In The Centre Spot

How does Eric Ashton fit into that classification? I would not suggest, nor would his greatest admirers claim, that he is the type of player who constantly dominates an occasion from the spectator's angle. Yet he certainly does so where his team-mates are concerned.

After all, no player who has captained Great Britain is exactly a nonentity. To some extent, Eric is a centre of the unobtrusive type, whose most effective moves are accomplished by stealth and secrecy, without any preliminary warning flourishes. They are finished off with deadly precision, either by personal effort or a pass to a colleague which sends him scampering over for a try.

How many of Billy Boston's most spectacular scoring moves, one wonders, have sprung from a piece of Ashton-inspired strategy?

It is Ashton's ability to 'read' a game; his uncannily perfect positional sense; and his perceptiveness in summing up the situation, defensively or aggressively, that makes him so fascinating a figure.

To a certain type of spectator who seeks only 'highlights' and glamour, Ashton may appear at times to be doing 'nothing' whereas in reality he is very much alive to every situation around him. He is constantly plotting and probing and, when things may be momentarily going against his side, planning a counter-move which, swift and decisive, turns the tables completely.

In this respect he is, perhaps, reminiscent of Jack Evans of Swinton's unrivalled 'Four Cups' side of the 'twenties. And while he lacks the latter's unique 'mesmeric' ability to baffle an opponent by a mere juggle of the ball, Ashton is comparably faster.

In his greatest moments Ashton can achieve an almost Gasnier-like elusiveness and brilliance. If these moments are, in the nature of things, less frequent than formerly, the fundamental skill remains unchallenged and among British centres, probably still unrivalled.

Moreover, lest it be thought that Eric is primarily an attacking player, to whom defensive measures are a secondary consideration, let me hasten to remove such illusions.

In a defensive situation Ashton is no less capable, cool-headed and courageous. In a tightly-fought finish he does not merely content himself with exhortations, leaving the donkey-work to others.

He is always in the thick of things, and thereby stamps himself as a player of character and courage, as well as one of abundant resource.

Long may Ashton continue to grace a sport to which he has given so generous a personal contribution, and so many moments of pleasure to his audiences.

Glory In The Centre Spot

ORIGINAL APPENDIX (5)

By Brian Batty of the *Daily Mail*

The date: January 8, 1960, probably means little to the most loyal Wigan fan today, but it nearly marked the end of an era at Central Park.

For it was the day Wigan almost waved good-bye to one of their greatest players ... Eric Ashton.

The day Wigan reluctantly agreed to place the Great Britain centre on the transfer at his own request at a fee of £13,000.

It is history now that eighteen days later Wigan and Ashton agreed to continue their famous partnership and the 'For Sale' signs were hurriedly pulled down at Central Park.

It would have spoiled a wonderful story if Ashton and Wigan had parted company, because their names have been synonymous in success.

For fans, the game over, are still talking about the latest and most memorable Cup Finals at Wembley.

No player could ask for a more exciting moment in his career than to carry off the Cup after such a classic contest, particularly after the big part Ashton had played in the conquest of Hunslet.

It was a Final overflowing with rich football, befitting the occasion, and the perfect setting and atmosphere for Ashton to show his real worth as a captain and a player.

Ashton has made his mark as far away as Australia, where fans have risen to his skill and sunk their loyalties.

But Wembley is the place most players would pick to produce their best form.

Ashton didn't steal the limelight as a lone star. He watched wisely every Hunslet thrust and then, when Wigan went on attack, pounced with decisive passes.

He speeded-up moves with the quick pass, pulled Hunslet's defence further apart with the shrewd long pass, and never missed a moment to try a surprise tactic.

Yet, like the best of captains, he stayed in the background when the game was won. He let other players savour the new taste of success.

Ashton's intelligent bearing on a game is immeasurable. For he rarely misses a mistake - even by his own players. And he wisely doesn't believe in trying to win Cup-ties before they are played.

Ask him who he thinks could be the most dangerous opposing player in a coming cup-tie and he will tell you: 'The match could be won by the player we least expect to do well, a lucky break or a silly mistake. Let's wait and see what happens.'

The game will be a lot poorer when Eric Ashton pulls on his jersey for the last time. But as long as he is connected with the game as a coach you can expect football based on *skill*.

Glory In The Centre Spot

144

AFTERWORD

NARLVI Interview with Eric Ashton
Recorded 29 March 2006, at The Aspull Village Club, Wigan
Producer/Interviewer: Leslie Smith

One of the most telling aspects of *Glory in the Centre Spot* is the extent to which its author, Eric Ashton, seems determined to stay out of it - the centre spot, that is.

Eric doesn't even tell us his date of birth - 24 January 1935. Nor does he reveal that, a spell doing National Service excepted, he lived in the family home at Mulberry Avenue until he was married at the age of 24.

Throughout *Glory in the Centre Spot* there are constant references to 'not being big-headed' and other such calls to modesty - a not uncommon trait when it comes to rugby league autobiographies. Most noticeably, it can't fail to strike the reader how so much of an already slim volume is devoted to the players Eric admired, rather than the life of the subject himself. The likes of Wigan icons Joe Egan and Billy Boston are paid handsome tribute, as might be expected, and there are also glowing testimonials to Vince Karalius, Alex Murphy and Brian McTigue. There is an obligatory 'World Team' selection, too, from a man who, quite clearly, felt more comfortable shining the light of glory on others. Maybe, that's why the original book contained so many testimonials from contemporary journalists. To gain any real sense of perspective on Eric Ashton the man, his ghost writers, Arthur Brooks and Malcolm Keogh, were apparently left with little choice but to call for outside help.

In preparing this latest edition of Eric's autobiography, we at Scratching Shed Publishing Ltd were faced with a similar problem. Imagine our delight, then, to discover an interview with Eric recorded in 2006, by the National Archive of Rugby League Video Interviews, an organisation to which rugby league owes an enormous debt of gratitude.

The NARLVI is an entirely self-funded enterprise that is determined to preserve the voices and stories of some of the greatest rugby league players of all time. As it says on their website - an advertisement for which appears later in this book - 'We have believed for some time that the great players of rugby league and their achievements should be captured on video for posterity.'

The result is a growing series of unmissable DVDs in which an array of rugby league greats share memories of their playing days and beyond. And, when faced with a video camera, under lights, those same players cannot help but reveal more of their personality and character than they might otherwise be willing or able, between the pages of a book. One such subject is Eric Ashton, who discusses many of the episodes accounted for in *Glory In The Centre Spot* (and occasionally contradicts factual details) while also talking about events that occurred subsequently to its publication.

What follows is a heavily abridged transcript of the above chat with Eric, published with the full co-operation and permission of the NARLVI. For a more in-depth interview, do please search out the original.

On that now legendary let-down by St. Helens:

My dad, Ernie, was a St. Helens fanatic and he would take me and my brother to the games, or we would sneak on at half-time, as you did in those days. My dad played ten or twelve first-team games for Warrington and his moment of glory came in one of those, when he found himself marking the great Alf Ellaby.

My dad wanted me to play rugby league when I left school and I did go up to St. Helens and train, but it was like a battlefield. If there was one, there must have been two hundred of us. That taught me a lesson right away. If you ever become a coach, don't run it like that. You can't watch two hundred people. It sounds silly, but there was always around a hundred, or one hundred and fifty people running around aimlessly, with the coaches saying 'do this' or 'do that'.

I learned that day that if you are a coach of the first team, the thing you have got to get right is to pick your best twenty people in the town. You have to take an interest in individuals and have no more than twenty to summer school. Find out their height, weight, where they live, what sort of family they have, and so on.

The people running it [at St. Helens] didn't know what was going on. I went home to my dad and he said: 'How have you got on? Did anybody speak to you?'

And I just said: 'nah, nobody's took me on.' 'Nobody's asked you anything?' 'No, no, no.' So he said: 'Carry on'. I did for about six weeks and then said: 'That's it.' 'Oh, give it another go.' 'No, I'm finished,' and that was it. After that, I didn't play at all until I went into the Army aged 18.

On playing for a home-town team:

I'll say this before I say anything. I cannot understand anybody who doesn't want to play for their home-town team. Now, I might be wrong because as the years went on, when I was coach at Wigan, I interviewed a number of Wigan-born players who went on to play for Warrington and all these places. I couldn't understand them. They had the chance to sign for Wigan. Some would say: 'Oh, they only sign top players and you won't get a chance.' I had all that thrown at me. But I still couldn't understand how me, as a coach, had asked them to sign but, no, they still went to other places. If I had been asked by St. Helens, I would have gone in a flash.

On being signed by Wigan:

It started with a bloke called Bert Marsh, who was a Wiganer and a club singer back home. I think he mentioned me to Billy Woods, who was a club director and the licensee of the Royal Oak pub in Wigan. He never said to me that he had, but I played for the Scottish Command up at Murrayfield one day and one of the lads came in and said: 'There are two men out there who want to speak to you and they are not allowed in here.'

So I went out and they asked me to sit in the car. It was Bill Gore and Billy Woods. It was January then and I was due out in the May. They asked me if I fancied joining Wigan. Best team in the world. Greatest name in the world. They gave me all the pack drill. And I said: '...aw, I don't know.' I said: 'I've been to one club, St. Helens, and got let down. I was just one of many and that won't happen again. I'm not that interested.'

'You must be interested,' they said. 'Well,' I said, 'let's see when I come out.' 'Oh, no, no no... just sign these forms here, like.' 'Oh," I said. 'I'm not signing anything. No, no. I'm not signing anything.' I had just turned 20. They wanted me to sign registration forms and play three trials; it was always about trials in those days.

I came out of the Army in May and Bobby Chisnall, who was a local lad, they got him to contact me. He said he'd meet me in the Town Hall square, so I got on the bus and that was the first time I went down. They asked me to sign for three [*sic*] trials and I thought, well, I've nothing to lose. So I did.

I went with Bobby to watch what they used to call the public trial matches, which was first team backs with 'A' team forwards and vice versa. It was a proper game and Wigan used to get eight or nine thousand watching that in them days. They would watch the grass grow; unbelievably keen. And I went down with Bobby to watch; it had nothing to do with the trials I had agreed.

The bloke who took the 'A' team came and said: 'Listen, how do you fancy a game?' I said: 'No, I've already signed for these three trials.' 'Oh,' he said, 'they won't judge you on this.' I said: 'I've not got my boots with me.' He said: 'We'll find you some boots.' I thought: 'Should I do it?' But I was extremely fit. I had just come out of the Army and you can be no fitter than that. Anyway, they put me on Ernie Ashcroft, who had just come off tour in '54-55, a great player, and I walked past him three or four times, no trouble at all. They whipped me off at half-time and talked me into signing. I signed for £125 [*sic*] and £37 of that went in tax, eventually. My dad wasn't best pleased - I was only 20 and hadn't got his permission. But I went straight into the first team and he ended up being delighted.

On captaincy:

I didn't believe in just throwing a coin up and saying that's me finished, and looking to the bench when a kick was vital. I did it.

I remember Joe Egan saying to me once, you should look to me. I said: 'Joe, if I have to look to you, get somebody else. I'm either doing it or I'm not.' A captain, I believe, is your coach on the field. I truly believe that. It's very important that you pick the right man. Not your best player, the right man who is a leader in his own right. And leaders are not always the best players. You need to be a thinker as a captain.

I had only been playing eighteen months when I took over the Wigan captaincy. Joe appointed me and from then on I was captain until I finished. They had made Don Platt - our full-back - captain, but in only the third game of the season he broke his leg against Leeds. I picked the papers up that night and everything was about how I had led the team after Don went off. Well, I don't think I led the team. As far as I was concerned, when Don went off, Ernie Ashcroft was captain. Anyway, Joe appointed me and I was captain from then on until I finished playing in 1969.

Although the coach had his input, I always liked to have my own two penn'orth before we went out and I let the players know what I expected. I think that was successful - I wouldn't have spent twelve years as captain if it hadn't been. Everybody has a right to play well or not to play well. You wouldn't go to watch sport if it always went according to plan. It doesn't work like that.

I'm not trying to be big-headed but, at times, I think that I could have been a better player if I had been playing for me and not going around rallying the team. As captain, there were things that you did in the game that put you out of position sometimes, and made you not take chances. We had a lot of people who liked to be individuals and possibly a lot who wouldn't have been as upset as me when we lost. But that's your make-up; that's what life's about.

You can upset some people easily, and there are some you could never upset, no matter what you said. I didn't just hate losing, I got upset about it. I could never understand why somebody wasn't as upset as me. If we'd come back from Bradford or somewhere and they got the cards out, I'd think: 'Cards?'. I always thought about the game. Some just played, went home, came back, trained, were told what to do and did it. I wasn't one of them. I took the game to heart. I had ambitions. One day, I wanted to captain Great Britain.

On personal publicity:

I got some good write-ups but, again, maybe that's because I was keener than all the others. I was so keen to do well. If you are given a chance take it - dad always used to drum that into us. That's what I wanted to do. I felt that I had a football brain. I could run a bit and didn't see why I couldn't make progress in the game.

You don't go around thinking: 'I'm a good 'un'. Well, I didn't. Everything I did, I thought I had to work at. There were tons of players with more natural ability than me. The Billy Bostons and Mick Sullivans of this world. I always felt that I could hold my place against anybody and compete against anybody individually, that never bothered me. But I did feel I had to be on my guard against those with more natural ability.

On Saints - Wigan rivalry:

Oh, I've had some stick in my life. You haven't enough film in these cameras for me to tell you how much stick I have had.

You've got to remember that I worked in St. Helens. Honestly, they used to eat and sleep rugby then. They would play on a Saturday afternoon and they would talk about it until the following Saturday, when they had another game. So imagine us losing, them winning and me going to work on a Monday morning. My dad got as much stick as I did.

My dad died in 1961 and so he wasn't around when I was appointed coach of St. Helens. He would have loved that. Oh, he would have loved that. That's life, isn't it?

On almost leaving Wigan (as a player):

I came very very close to playing for St. Helens, when I had a bit of an upset at Wigan in 1961. I can't think what it was about now, but it was something I didn't agree with and I just said: 'Ah well, I'll have a move then.' So they said: 'St. Helens have tapped you, haven't they?' I said: 'No, they've not,' and they hadn't. So they put me on the transfer list at £13,000, which was about £8,000 more than anyone had ever been on before. Well, nobody had that money. Saints went to £11,000. It was Tom Mitchell of Workington who spoiled it for me. Where I could object to the fee, if I'd been on a month, I couldn't object if someone was willing to pay it. And Tom, who was the Great Britain tour manager in 1958, came over and had a chat with me about going to Cumbria. I told him I wouldn't go up there but he still put the offer in to Wigan of £13,000, which stopped me from getting it reduced. So I eventually had to go cap in hand and come off. But I got as near as that to going to St. Helens. The fee was too big.

On the lack of security, even for great players:

I remember once at Central Park, we were playing Leeds, and Brian McTigue was changed. He was always one for getting changed early, Brian, and he would sit there reading the programme.

He hadn't trained on the Thursday, so I said: 'I thought you weren't playing?' 'Oh aye,' he said. 'If I miss this and you win, I'll not get in next week.'

This is Brian McTigue, a man of his standing. And I looked at his foot and, do you know, his toes were blue. He had pulled that strapping so hard that he couldn't feel it, and he played. You would never do that today. It's a tale that takes some believing, but it's true. His toes were blue, he was strapped that tight, but he was feared of missing [the game] because it was not uncommon to have a couple of internationals on the bench. It's a tale worth telling because [someone like Brian] who should have been guaranteed his place, week in, week out, whatever the results, even he thought that he had to play and play well to keep in. That was his example - not a good example, he could have lost his foot through it, but he did it.

On going into coaching with Wigan:

I went into coaching shortly after coming back from Australia [in 1962]. A chap from Eastern Suburbs actually flew to Wigan to make me an offer. He had got it into his head that if he made me an offer I would go and play there. The Rugby League immediately put a ban on players going to Australia, though, so that scotched it anyway.

Anyway, Wigan made me an offer to be player-coach. And when the time came in 1963 for me to take over, one of things they said was that they didn't want me playing for Great Britain.

In those days, the Great Britain team was picked a fortnight in advance and if you didn't play on the Saturday before the match you had to cry off. You had to play to prove you were fit. Then you went for a medical on the Monday, where you all met, and if you passed that you went into camp for the week. [The Wigan board] said that if they were giving me the job full-time, I had to be with the Wigan players and not Great Britain, and I accepted it. I rue the day that I did. I was in my prime, only 27, and I think I took too much on to start with. To be player-coach of a club like Wigan was a bit much.

I had played in twenty-seven Tests in six years, so I don't know how many more I could have played in. It's something I'll never know now. Twenty-seven is no age. Alex Murphy played against New Zealand when he was 31.

But I'd made my decision. Well, they made the decision for me, as they always did, and I went along with it.

The encouragement for me was going full-time as well. I thought that may not come around again. I was working in the glassworks then, but they always had a full-time coach,

Wigan. When I first went there, Ted Ward was the coach, a big Welsh centre. Then Joe Egan came and then Jim Sullivan. It was always full-time. They actually had a full-time masseur, too. They just tried to do things that little bit better, Wigan. If you got injured you could always have treatment.

The biggest problem I had was that players who I had played six or seven years with were coming to the end. As I say, I was 27 or 28 then, Billy Boston was a bit older than me, McTigue two years older than me, and I knew that evil day would come when I would have to leave Billy and Mac out, and other players before them. That was one of the biggest strains on me. Taking a team that I had played with for so many years, being responsible for it, and then it coming to the time when it needed replacing. I found that difficult, but I had been given the job and I got on with it .

It didn't happen, with Billy, until late on. We were both about to finish anyway by that time and Billy finished in 1968. I finished playing in 1969, so that worked itself out. But it was always there in the back of my mind that it could happen, and also with Brian. In fact, Brian did me a favour. He winked at me and said: 'I've had enough now'.

All in all, I just got on with it and we had a fair amount of success. We won the Challenge Cup in 1965 against Hunslet, went to finals, topped the league in 1970. Well, I lasted ten years, so I must have done something right.

On his brief stint as coach of Leeds:

I finished playing in 1969 then I carried on the coaching until 1973. After that, I went to Leeds for twelve months. Well, I went to Leeds for three months really. Having been with Wigan for ten years, I was 39 and thought that I had better get out of this game full-time. I thought I could see that the game didn't lend itself to being full-time. Wigan's gates had gone from 20,000 to 10,000, and then even 8-9,000. I thought it would come to Wigan that they didn't want a full-time coach.

I was offered another deal but I thought, no, I'll have to get another job sooner or later, and I was going on 40. So I gave them notice in the January and they didn't like it. They said, what are you telling us now for? So I said: 'I just thought I'd be fair. Gives you time to look around and see who you want.' Anyway it went on and we weren't in good spirits with each other for a while. They kept coming back and offering me this and that but I said no. They never offered me coaching part-time and they knew that was what I wanted. They believed they had to have a full-time coach.

We drew Leeds at Leeds in the first round of the Cup that year, 1973, and we won 28-8 or something like that, and Jack Myerscough and the chief executive, Alf Rutherford, came in the players bar after the game for a drink and said: 'Where are you going?' I said: 'I've got no work.' They said: 'Give over.' I said: 'No I haven't. I'm leaving Wigan to get another job out of the game because if there's no full-time coaching, I'm only 39 and I've got to earn a living. If I am going to make a move, I need to make it now.' And they said: 'What would you say if we said we were interested.' I said: 'What, part-time?' And they said: 'Yeah.' Derek Turner was their coach then. And from then on they just kept phoning and I was playing hard to get saying can you find me a job then? They said: 'Yeah, we'll find you a job. What about repping for a brewer?' They fixed me up with an interview with a fellow at Webster's brewery in Halifax. Webster's were part of Wilson's in Manchester and, because I didn't want to move to Yorkshire, I ended up being given a job there instead. I repped the St Helens, Southport and Widnes areas. So I did get my job and I went to Leeds.

But the motorway only went up to Huddersfield then and... oh, that first year. It was the miners strike, 1974. I'd get there in hail or rain or snow, over the moors, and when I got there, there were no lights because the power cuts were on. We would run around in the dark at training.

Everything got me down. I would come back over the

moors and it would be foggy. I took my youngster, Beverley, with me on one particular day. She was crying and wanted to come, but she was frightened on the way home so I thought, I can't carry on with this. I stuck it for the season and then rang Alf up saying that I couldn't continue. 'Well, you know best,' he said. I told him that I hadn't been tapped up and wasn't going anywhere else and, if I was, I would stay out of the game for the two years I had promised that I should have been coach. 'Oh, don't you worry about that,' he said. Unbelievable.

I came off the phone, went home, and Saints were there. They said: 'How are you fixed for coaching? I said: 'You won't believe it - but I have just packed my Leeds job in.' They said: 'We want you here. I said: 'Listen, you will not believe this but I have just packed in with Leeds, for no reason other than travelling. It's getting me down with the job and everything, I can't do both.' They said: 'Well ring them up and see what they say.' So I said: 'Okay, I'll not give you my word now, but I will ring them.' So I rang Alf and he said: 'Don't worry about it.' I said: 'I would hate you to think that I have known this all along, and that I could just go from Leeds to St Helens, because I wouldn't do that.' I told him that, as far as I was concerned, the twelve months I did at Leeds were among the happiest I'd had in the game. I said I was quite happy to see out the two years and if there was anything doing at that point, I'd take it then. Alf said: 'No, you take it.' So I did and was there six years then as coach.

On coaching St. Helens:

I had picked the team myself at Leeds, and I also did that at St. Helens.

I didn't always pick the team at Wigan. I submitted a team at Wigan. The directors always had the right to change it, which was frustrating because I then had to go down and tell that player that he wasn't selected after all. I couldn't say to him: 'I've picked you but they've took you out,' because that would have soon got back to the board. That I couldn't do. Anyway, at Leeds and then St. Helens I picked the team with no interference whatsoever.

St. Helens wasn't like Leeds, though. They never had any money. Even in them days, you struggled. There were one or two players I wanted, particularly from Wigan. There was Eddie Cunningham, who was a great player, and Bill Francis, who I thought could do our club a bit of good. I knew what would be said. Some of the board said: 'Hey, don't be fetching Wiganers here. We're not going to be overrun by Wiganers, are we?' So I said: 'No you're not. You're going to have two very good players.' And they did turn out to be two very good players.

They didn't look at the player, they looked at the club, but it has always been like that with Wigan and St. Helens. I believe it's like that with Leeds and Bradford too. Well, that was the feeling I got at Leeds. If we were going to win two games, make it Bradford home and away. Mind you, there wasn't quite the same resistance to transfers between the clubs. I have been at St Helens for thirty-four years in total. I have been there since 1976 and when I finished coaching I joined the board.

On the importance of a player's character:

Character has a lot to do with who you sign. You shouldn't just sign a person because they can play rugby a bit. Particularly as a lad, you should look at his parents and see how he has been brought up, because you can have a lot of trouble at a club when someone doesn't toe the line and respect discipline.

Character is very important. There are some magnificent lads at St Helens at the moment; Paul Sculthorpe, Sean Long... I know that he got into trouble with that betting, but you wouldn't get a better lad than Sean Long. Scully too.

Glory In The Centre Spot

Character has always been crucial. If you've not got the right attitude and don't work hard enough, then you won't make it, no matter how much ability you've got. And that is as true today as it was in our day.

In those days, we didn't have all the TV cameras that we have now and that was one of the big disadvantages in my coaching days. I would say to a player: 'You've not done this, ' or 'you've not done that'. They would deny it and I had no proof. It was your word against his. The only thing in your favour was that you picked the team and he didn't, but to be able to sit them down and show them what you are talking about now must be marvellous. That's something to be envied.

In closing:

I count myself very lucky for what I achieved because, as far as I am concerned, you can only be so dedicated if the woman you married and the kids you've got supported you, and mine did. My wife, Doreen, not only followed me to home games, she took the two kids with her. It makes life easier and you can't play any sport at the top level if you're not happy at home.

I joined the board of St Helens in 1982. That was always a bit strange, having been a player and a coach and now on the 'other side'. But even though I have been a coach myself, I have never tried to lean or put pressure on any coach while I have been a director at Saints. I appreciate their difficulties. If you've worn the T-shirt, as they say, you realise the problems that there are in anything.

You don't get many players who are interested in being on a board, but I have just been interested in rugby league all my life. I started in 1955 and I have never been out of it. My life has been rugby league.

Glory In The Centre Spot

EPILOGUE

By Dave Hadfield
Originally published as part of 'Icons of League'
Rugby League World magazine, May 2008

Everyone knows that Eric Ashton was a great centre and captain and that he commanded just as much respect as a coach and a chairman.

The game's first MBE and one of the few men held in equal affection in Wigan and St. Helens – most people know that as well.

But I needed a couple of reminders recently to confirm what a central role he played in the last fifty years or so of rugby league – why he is an icon, in other words.

The first involved a trawl of my bookshelves. There I found that the earliest player autobiography I could lay my hands on was not by Murphy or Karalius, Boston or Fox. The one man thought to have sales potential at a time when there was a prevalent suspicion that many rugby league fans could not read was Eric Ashton, whose *Glory in the Centre Spot* was published in 1966.

My second-hand copy used to belong to the Seafarers' Education Service and looks as though it spent some time underwater. It's pleasant to imagine sailors from distant shores browsing through it in their hammocks – if they hadn't been phased out by the mid-sixties.

Another memory goes back fifteen years or so, to when a London theatre staged a revival of *The Changing Room*, a play that was David Storey's curtain-raiser or training run for *This Sporting Life*. There was a banner draped across the façade of the theatre, showing a player pinning his ears back and running.

It was not a current player, though, and there were some at the time who would have looked pretty good up there. It was Eric Ashton, *circa* 1958, in his Great Britain shirt. Nothing that had happened in the thirty-odd years since had produced an image that said Rugby League At Its Best more eloquently.

The bare facts of his playing career are evocative enough. Rejected by St. Helens – a couple of streets from his home - after one 'B' team game, he was scouted in the Army by Wigan, played one trial match and signed for £150.

In his autobiography, Ashton feels, like a lot of players of his generation, that he signed too cheaply.

'Right then I had one pound in my pocket. With that kind of money behind you, £150 sounds like the crock of gold. I signed... and I've never stopped kicking myself since.'

Neither that nor his initial status as a reluctant winger boded well for the long-term relationship between player and club, but once Joe Egan had arrived as coach and moved him to centre the stage was set for one of the great Wigan careers.

His total of 497 appearances puts him behind only Jim Sullivan, Ken Gee and the man he replaced, Ernie Ashcroft. His 231 tries are only bettered by Messrs Boston, Ring,

Nordgren, Leytham and Ashcroft. His 448 goals put him in the top ten and only Sullivan, Farrell and Tyrer have scored more than his 1589 points.

Amid that little lot, he captained Wigan at Wembley five times and won 26 Great Britain caps. It is a remarkable record, but the numbers do not come anywhere near telling the whole story.

His career record was achieved in style, as a centre of the rapier type, rather than the broadsword.

Take the description [republished in this volume] from one WR Sinclair of the *Sunday Mirror*, a pressman venerable enough to have seen Billy Batten and Harold Wagstaff and to be able to compare them with Ashton:

> "I would not suggest, nor would his greatest admirers claim, that he is the type of player who constantly dominates an occasion from the spectator's angle. Yet he certainly does so where his team-mates are concerned.
>
> "....Eric is a centre of the unobtrusive type, whose most effective moves are accomplished by stealth and secrecy, without any preliminary warning flourishes.
>
> They are finished off with deadly precision, either by personal effort or a pass to a colleague that sends him scampering over for a try."

Which leads us neatly to Billy Boston, the number one beneficiary of those skills. If there has ever been a better centre-wing combination, for club and country, than these two, then it has been a very well-kept secret.

There is no way of quantifying it now, but a very high proportion of Billy's 478 tries for Wigan must have been directly traceable to Eric. That was what centres did in those days, but not many did it like Ashton.

'I don't think any pair will score over 600 tries together,

like we did,' says Boston – surely one of rugby league's least risky predictions.

'Wigan found him in the Army in Scotland after Saints had turned him down – what a mistake that was.

'At the time, Jack Broome was my centre and Eric started off on the left wing. The next season, he was my centre and we got on pretty good from the start.

'He was so smooth and cool and collected. He never got ruffled; he was out of this world to play with.

'He used to dummy to me sometimes and go himself. He didn't give me the ball when there was nothing on, or let me take all the knocks.'

So well-oiled was their right-wing partnership that it comes as a surprise now for Billy to insist that they did no special work to hone it.

'We didn't used to rehearse anything. It was just instinct. I knew what he was going to do and he knew what I was going to do.'

The one exception to that was a move Wigan – and later Great Britain – used to work with the scrum, with Boston coming in to hit the ball from deep outside the stand-off. It was a move that had no name.

'Eric would just give me a look and I'd know it was on. It used to work as well.'

The instinctive understanding between the two was helped by the way that they always got on so well together off the pitch.

'We were together for twelve years at Wigan and we never had a wrong world or a falling out,' he recalls.

'We went out together every Saturday night. Eric would go back to St. Helens after the match and we'd meet up in Wigan with our wives.'

Not that their friendship made Eric a soft touch for Billy when he was Wigan captain.

'He was a brilliant captain, but if he'd something to say to you, he'd say it.

'I remember one game – I think it was at Hull – when I went and told him that I'd broken my finger.

'"You're not going off," he said.

'"I didn't say I was," I said

'"Well, what are you telling me for?"'

Ah, yes, the sentimental, caring, sharing world of rugby league in the 1950s.

Even by that time, Saints were all too well aware that they had made what Boston calls 'one hell of a mistake' by letting Ashton slip through their fingers and made periodic attempts to put it right and team him up with Tom Van Vollenhoven in a combination that might have been able to give Boston and Ashton a run for its money.

Wigan succeeded in pricing Ashton out of a move. On the one occasion when they did express a willingness to sell him, there was a conveniently higher bid on the table from Workington Town, which effectively put paid to any transfer talk.

Ashton was also coach in his final seasons before retiring as a player in 1968, before carrying on purely in a coaching capacity and then having one season in charge at Leeds.

In 1974, more than twenty years after turning him down, Saints finally brought him home and got an almost immediate reward when he guided them to what was, remarkably, their one and only First Division title the following season.

Equally memorable was the way his supposedly over-the-hill side beat Widnes in the 'Dads' Army' Cup final at Wembley in 1976. The aura he had as a player still surrounded his as a coach, in which capacity he also led Great Britain and England between 1978 and 1980.

'His uncanny ability to read a game made him a natural coach,' wrote Saints historian, Alex Service, in an appreciation in their match-day programme.

If his contribution had ended there and then, he would still have been a towering figure in the history of two great clubs. In 1996, however, he became unique when he led out Saints against Bradford at Wembley, becoming the first man to preside over a Cup final victory as captain, coach and chairman.

Later that same year, he saw his club become the first to win a daring new venture called Super League. He had spanned all the eras separating that revolution from the days when great players were recruited from their National Service.

His coach that year, Shaun McRae, would speak for many in describing him as the ideal chairman, willing to let you get on with the job, but ready with advice when needed.

Turbulent times lay ahead in the Knowsley Road boardroom, but, even when his time in the chair was over, Eric remained a voice of sanity amid the intermittent madness in his role as club president.

I recall his bemusement at some of the clashing egos he witnessed; genuine bemusement, because an over inflated sense of his own importance was something he never developed.

He was vitally important to Saints, though, as an embodiment of the decency and gentlemanliness that still lie at the heart of a game that can be so brutal on the pitch.

In 2005, he was belatedly inducted into the Rugby League Hall of Fame, an honour to stand alongside his MBE.

By that time, he was already fighting a long and dignified battle against the cancer that finally claimed him.

Typically, he did not let it keep away from many matches. Every time you saw him at Knowsley Road, he was that little bit more gaunt and frail, but still recognisably the giant of the game he had always been and still a fount of common sense.

His passing was marked, with a rare appropriateness, by a minute's silence before the Good Friday derby between the two clubs he served with such distinction.

Perhaps the most poignant moment, though, was at

Wigan's next home game, where the mourning was led by his old partner in crime, Billy Boston.

Alright, it wasn't Central Park, the stage on which they created so much havoc and carved out so many tries, but the idea was undeniably the right one.

'The chairman asked me to go out on the pitch to remember Eric,' he says. 'I was proud to do that.'

Those who knew him far less well, but who respected him just as much, can be proud too of their association with one of the great men of rugby league.

Glory In The Centre Spot

168

PERSONAL TRIBUTE

By Denis Whittle
St Helens RLFC historian and lifelong friend of Eric Ashton

It could be construed as a masterpiece of understatement to say that rugby league has been an integral part of my life, right from the day I first set foot on Knowsley Road during the dark days of World War Two.

Journalistic jaunts to the Southern Hemisphere and to every ground in the English competition have been garnished with great players and matches, plus - as befits the family game - friendships that have stood the test of time.

For me, pride of place in that latter category must go to peerless prince of centres, Eric Ashton. Being of similar vintage to myself, Eric and I first became acquainted at Rivington Road school, St. Helens.

Over the halcyon days that followed, I remained on first-name terms with Eric's family, in particular Doreen, his wife since 1958, daughters Michelle and Beverley, grandchildren Alexandra and Ryan Liptrot, and Victoria and Greg Smith.

Family affair ... Eric with the Ashton family upon his entry into rugby league's Hall of Fame in 2005. Flanking Eric and his wife, Doreen, are grandsons Greg Smith and Ryan Liptrot. In front are Alexandra Liptrot and Victoria Smith (granddaughters), and Beverley Smith and Michelle Huyton (daughters)

Oval ball starlets Ryan and Greg (a mirror image of Eric) are chips off the old block. For along with sharing the guiding influence of their famous grandfather, they are also the sons of ex-Saints players Graham Liptrot and John Smith.

At the time of Eric's death from cancer in March 2008, his broken-hearted daughter Bev said: 'Dad was a loving husband, fantastic father and wonderful grandad. We will treasure his memory for ever.'

An impeccably observed minute's silence was undertaken before the Saints versus Wigan derby game, appropriately enough, on Good Friday that year.

In his heyday, the debonair self-effacing Eric - standing at 6ft 1in and tipping the scale at 14 stone - was a threequarter cast in the classical mould. He was blessed with pace, handling ability, tactical know-how and an uncanny ability to read a game. All this plus leadership flair too.

As I am sure readers of his autobiography will agree, Eric's lifetime in the 13-a-side code makes for a compelling story. It's all in there. His rugby league baptism under the watchful eye of sportsmaster Mr. 'Polly' Byron at 'Rivvy Road' school, just a drop-kick's distance from Eric's Mulberry Avenue home and Saints' stadium. Town and county selection at schoolboy level. Most famous, perhaps, is the tale of how Eric trained with Saints alongside the likes of Walter Delves and Bill Boycott but, remarkably in view of what the future held, was not snapped up by the Knowsley Road board.

As we now know, Saints' loss would turn out to be Wigan's gain. Prescient Central Park directors, Bill Gore and Billy Woods, handed Eric a contract after he starred in a rugby union game at Murrayfield while on National Service in the Royal Artillery.

All in all, Ashton was to appear in 497 games for Wigan in which he scored 231 tries and landed 448 goals before taking a well-earned retirement in 1969. His testimonial match featured Wigan-born versus St. Helens-born squads (the latter including Eric!) at Central Park on Whit Monday of that year.

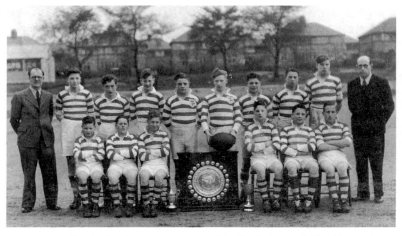

Rivington Road school team ... winners of the Daily Dispatch Shield in 1949.
Eric is on the extreme left of the back row.

Glory In The Centre Spot

In the international arena, Eric Ashton earned 26 Test caps (15 of them as captain) between 1957 and 1963, and was a member of the Ashes-winning squads in Australia in 1958 and 1962, becoming the first St. Helens-born skipper on that second tour. In addition Eric also figured in the Great Britain World Cup parties of 1957 and 1960, when he led the victorious side in that latter encounter.

Meanwhile, during his golden age at Wigan, Eric forged a lethal right-wing partnership with fellow legend Billy Boston, now etched indelibly into rugby league folklore. Always the most sporting of players, he was sent for an early bath just once, in a home game with Leeds in 1961. That followed a breach of the peace with fearsome 'Farmer' Jack Fairbank, who was also dismissed.

Eric captained the 'Cherry and Whites' in a record six Wembley finals, including those against

Legendary partnership ... Eric Ashton and Billy Boston with the Challenge Cup

Saints in 1961 and 1966. It was during that momentous year that he and Doreen were guests of the Queen at Buckingham Palace, with the award of his MBE coinciding with the initial publication of this book, his life-story, *Glory in the Centre Spot*.

When that book ended, though, another equally successful story began to unfold, this time in suit and tie, rather than rugby league kit.

Following a coaching stint with Wigan, Eric then took up a similar role at Headingley with Leeds. But when the

172

Honoured by the Queen ... Eric and Doreen Ashton at Buckingham Palace in 1966
when the former Great Britain captain was presented with his MBE.

travelling became a bind, he returned to his St. Helens roots
after being head-hunted by chairman Harry Cook and
secretary Basil Lowe in 1974.

With Eric as coach, silverware soon began to land on the
Saints sideboard. The Championship 'pot' was lifted in 1975,
while the Challenge Cup, Premiership and Floodlit Trophies
were all won during the next season. A Premiership encore
arrived in 1977, followed by a 14-12 Wembley defeat to
Leeds twelve months later, prior to Eric handing the
coaching reins over to Kel Coslett in 1979-80.

Even then, Eric's service to rugby league was far from
over. An invitation to join the board of St Helens came in 1982
and the by-now silver-thatched Ashton - who had supported
Saints since his boyhood - remained at Knowsley Road from
that moment on. He was the epitome of loyalty and a revered
ambassador, both for club and rugby league in general, in
both hemispheres for more than fifty years all in all.

Fittingly, Eric also occupied the hot seat of chairman at

Glory In The Centre Spot

Up for the Cup ... Wigan skipper Eric Ashton proudly holds the Challenge Cup aloft after a 13-9 victory over Workington Town in 1958.

At the double ... St Helens won both the Challenge Cup and Super League trophy in 2001, which naturally found the board of directors in celebratory mood. At the rear are Arthur Thomas and Joe Spencer. In front, *left to right*: Eamonn McManus, Eric Ashton, Howard Morris (chairman), Malcolm Kay and Tom Ellard

Saints from 1993-1997, twice leading the side out ahead of the Wembley conquests of Bradford Bulls in 1996 and 1997. In doing so, he became the only man to captain, coach and be chairman of Challenge Cup winning teams. He was also at the helm when Saints lifted the inaugural summer Super League title in 1996.

By common consent Eric Ashton was a true sportsman who earned the respect of all who played with or against him. Given his sky-high pedigree, including life membership of the Rugby Football League and presidency of Saints, it was inevitable that he should be bestowed with the code's ultimate Hall of Fame accolade in 2005.

As his former threequarter partner, Billy Boston, once reflected: 'Great player, centre and gentleman. What more can one say about Eric Ashton? He started as a winger but it was a lucky day or me, Wigan and Great Britain when 'Ash' moved into the centre spot.'

Personally, I feel honoured to have known Eric since his

Proud Englishman ... Eric Ashton and Keith Barnes lead out England and Australia during the 1959 Ashes series. *Picture courtesy Rugby League Journal.*

short-pants days and, in more recent times, at Sprayhurst Social Club, St. Helens, on Thursday evenings. Anecdotal tales abound regarding his 'chairmanship' of the club's rugby league debating society, even when his health began to fail. Despite Eric's physical absence, the society continues to scrum down at this popular watering hole. Its grey-beard membership includes Eric's elder brother Ernie, Johnny Fishwick, Alf Arnold and George Walker (late of Rochdale Hornets, Warrington and Liverpool Stanley respectively).

Add to that venerable lot Arthur Briers (father of Warrington 's Lee), plus mine host Terry Loughlin (Test centre Paul is his son), and it is almost superfluous to say that the oval ball is regularly out with a vengeance at a venue where distinguished Eric Ashton held his weekly court for so long.

And as those stars of bygone days were busy chewing the rugby league cud, their women-folk were studiously

Life President ... Eric and Doreen Ashton with, *left to right*, daughters Michelle
Huyton and Beverley Smith, and Beverley's son Greg, when Eric's long service at
St Helens was recognised with the club's ultimate accolade.
Unless otherwise stated, all pictures in this chapter courtesy of Denis Whittle

scrutinising their bingo cards in the next room, while Eric
looked forward to welcoming BBC Radio Merseyside
commentator Alan Rooney to the Ashton abode for their
regular tête-à-tête the following morning.

It was at those weekly Friday get-togethers that Eric's
better half 'Doe', as he fondly dubbed her, would serve a
strictly non-alcoholic brew, given that the early-morning
dew would still be on the Ashtons' well-manicured lawn
when raconteur Rooney set off on his return journey to
Billinge two hours later.

As for Mrs. Ashton, she has been greatly comforted
following the loss of Eric by the messages of support from
all points of the rugby league compass. Further evidence, if
any were needed, that the code of rugby league has fully
honoured its proud boast of being one big family affair.

ERIC ASHTON

TESTIMONIAL MATCH
ST. HELENS BORN XIII
v
WIGAN BORN XIII

CENTRAL PARK
WIGAN

WHIT MONDAY, 26th MAY, 1969
Kick-off 7-30 p.m.

SOUVENIR PROGRAMME   ONE SHILLING

179

Glory In The Centre Spot

KEN BROOME *Chairman of Wigan R.L. Club.*

No player, however great, can expect to go on for ever. But at a time when we are being told constantly that star personalities in our game are becoming even rarer season by season, the retirement of Billy Boston and Eric Ashton within ten months of each other is a double loss which the Wigan Club can ill afford. And the game is all the poorer, too.

I will always remember Eric Ashton as the lad who was signed on the strength of half a trial game and then emerged as a supreme footballer, a great captain and, at all times, a gentleman.

In 14 seasons, since his debut for us in August, 1955, he has shown a remarkable consistency. Never once in all those seasons has he played in our "A" team.

Eric has always proved himself a great leader, both of Wigan and Great Britain. Like anybody else of his calibre, he has had his off days. Yet somehow the directors always felt that much more confident when he was out on that field leading the team — even on the occasion when he had reported that he wasn't feeling "too good."

Our only bit of bother hit the headlines. When we transfer-listed Eric for £13,000 — which was an astronomical figure then — we were convinced that St. Helens would be sourely tempted. They didn't take the bait. This was our good fortune. And I suspect that the Saints' still haven't stopped regretting it."

Eric Ashton will always be remembered by R.L. followers the world over for his part in the incomparable partnership with Bill Boston. But Wiganers know him as a truly great player in his own right. My directors and I sincerely hope that tonight Eric gets the type of send off he deserves.

★   ★   ★

WIGAN FOOTBALL CLUB LIMITED

Directors:

Mr. L. K. BROOME (Chairman)	Mr. H. GOSTELOW
Mr. W. WOOD (Vice-Chairman)	Mr. J. HILTON
Mr. W. ACKERS	Mr. M. RYAN
Mr. S. BAXENDALE	Mr. A. E. WALLS
Mr. N. BIBBY	Mr. H. S. WEBSTER

Secretary: Mr. G. SUTCLIFFE

Coach: Mr. E. ASHTON   Telephone: Wigan 43079

Cover picture : Wigan v Wakefield Trinity, R.L.C.C. Final at Wembley, 1963

A word of

Thanks

from

Eric . . .

First of all I would like to thank the **Wigan directors** for granting permission for me to use **Central Park** for my Testimonial match.

I would also like to thank everyone who has helped in the organisation of this game. Without their help I would have been unable to arrange this game or at least my task would have been much more difficult. With special thanks to **Marion Green,** the assistant secretary who has been a very big help.

Also to all the clubs for granting permission for their players to play in my game and also to the players themselves for readily agreeing to participate on my behalf.

Last but not least I would like to thank you — the spectators — for coming to see this game and for your loyal support which you have given — not only to me — but to the **Wigan Club** and to **Rugby League** in general.

HIGHLIGHTS OF ERIC ASHTON'S CAREER

During Eric Ashton's illustrious career in Rugby League over the last fourteen years he has made 501 appearances, scored over 300 tries and kicked over 450 goals for the Wigan Club. Added to this Eric has lead the Wigan team out at Wembley on 6 occasions and under his leadership the Wigan team has won every honour which is possible. He has also helped Great Britain and Lancashire to many victories with some excellent goals and many tries. Eric toured Australia on three occassions which were the World Cup Tour to Australia in 1957, again in 1958 and in 1962 he captained the Great Britain Touring Team. He also captained the Great Britain team in the World Cup Competition which was played in this country in 1960. In addition Eric has represented Lancashire and Great Britain on many occasions against France and New Zealand. Apart from his footballing honours he has also been honoured with yet another. This being the fact that he is the only Rugby League player ever to receive the M.B.E. from Her Majesty the Queen at Buckingham Palace for his services to Rugby League.

181

Glory In The Centre Spot

BILL FALLOWFIELD, O.B.E., M.A., *Secretary of the Rugby Football League.*

When the history of the Rugby League game is eventually written, fitting tributes will be paid to many of the great players who have adorned the Rugby fields of the world.

Foremost amongst these names will be that of Eric Ashton, M.B.E., of Wigan.

Wigan — and Great Britain for that matter — have every reason to feel proud of the prowess Eric Ashton invariably showed in all games . . . for his club, his county and his country.

He set a truly wonderful example of skill and sportsmanship which the youth of the country, who hold an interest not only in our game but in all sports, would do well to follow.

HAROLD MATHER (Guardian) *who is Chairman of the Rugby League Writers' Association.*

We all grow old sometime, but the loss to Wigan, in particular, and to the game in general through Eric Ashton deciding the time has come to hang up his boots makes one wish that some exception to that rule were possible. As unfortunately, it is not, what can one say about Eric that has not been said countless times before?

A gentleman off the field as well as on it, he soon became both renowned and respected for his fair play as much as for his skill and shrewd captaincy. Not surprisingly, therefore, that skill rightly was appreciated the world over. Indeed, legion are the times Eric's eye for an opening, his speed off the mark, and his skill combined to bewilder opponents.

182

But I wonder if, when the time comes for reminiscing, he will look back on anything with more personal pride and pleasure than the tour of Australia in 1962, for then, as I was privileged to report at the time, he not only captained a fine side splendidly but played no small part in what was a most successful tour. Certainly Eric will be missed on the Rugby League fields of the world; may his influence as a coach now blossom and so keep his name fresh in our minds.

JOE HUMPHREYS (Daily Mirror).

Summer Rugby ... Two divisions — some suggest three ... four or six tackles. Such proposed changes may help bring back some of the Rugby League's missing fans. But the foundation for any major rise in attendances surely demands finding the Eric Ashton's of the future. The talented gentlemen of Rugby League.

Players who can stride through the roughest and toughest game in the world fairly and honourably and always be a delight to watch. Eric will always have a place in my Top 10 of Rugby League players. He has been one of the truly greats in post war rugby.

The Rugby League could have had no finer ambassador and as he closes his 14 seasons as a Wigan player, St. Helens must still wonder how they failed to spot his potential as he trained with their players before finally signing for Wigan.

Wigan certainly scored that day. The Rugby League can score tomorrow. Never mind the revolutionary ideas to ginger up public interest ... scour the junior fields of Lancashire, Yorkshire and Cumberland for the Eric Ashton's of the future. They are a must.

JACK BENTLEY (Daily Express).

Twelve years ago last month a 22-year-old Eric Ashton was a shock choice for Great Britain's squad for the second World Cup tourney taking place in Australia. At the time, Eric told me: "I had never even thought about being selected. I am thrilled and delighted."

But that was the start of an international Rugby Leaue career which bears comparison with any in the history of the game. It has not been my pleasure, anyway, to watch a more complete player in action over the past twenty years.

Even recently at the comparatively ripe "old" football ages of 33 and 34 Ashton, the only player to be awarded the M.B.E. for his services to the game, has been adorning the matches in which he played with superb football to show up his younger adversaries — and colleagues.

I know of no player in the game who has been as respected as Ashton, both by team mates and opponents all over the Rugby League world. He is regarded in Australasia as one of the best skippers ever to lead a touring team.

I cannot recall any other player who was as fair minded about opponents as Eric Ashton. He was never one to squeal no matter how hard it might have been to take defeat and I only hope that somewhere he can find a protege to mould in his own image for the benefit of Rugby League fans of the future.

Chairman Mr. Webster introducing Eric to Mr. Harold Wilson, Prime Minister on the occasion of the St. Helens v Wigan, R.L.C.C. Final at Wembley in 1966

185

EDDIE WARING (Sunday Mirror and B.B.C.).

I was never more impressed by Eric Ashton than when I saw him in action in Australia in 1962. There have been many good players in this country, but you have to be a great player to shine in the hurly-burly of an Australian tour. In 1962 he had the added responsibility of being captain and he was the only man I know who could keep control of players like Alec Murphy and the older men such as Vince Karalius and Dick Huddart. They looked up to Eric because they respected him.

I remember particularly his disappointment after the British touring team in 1962 were prevented from making a clean sweep of the Test matches by that doubtful Irvine try. But Eric Ashton came back, although he wasn't fit, to help slam Sydney St. George in a match where he broke his ankle.

Ashton has epitomised the professional footballer as much as anyone I know and as far as captains are concerned, I put him on a par with such greats as Gus Risman, Ernest Ward, Alan Prescott and Dickie Williams.

It's been a pleasure to know him and I wish him every success in the future.

PAUL HARRISON (Sun).

Eric Ashton's playing days are over, but although it is sad to see him finally hanging up his boots, I'm not sorry. For Eric is packing up while he is still worthy of a place in any team — remember that game against St. Helens a month ago — and he will now never be regarded as a fallen idol.

Whenever the conversation turns to Rugby League the name of Eric Ashton is bound to crop up and that is tribute in itself to a man who has graced the game so magnificently for so long.

Unfortunately, I only saw Ashton play in the twilight of his career, but although he might have lost some of his speed, he'd lost none of his tactical ability — an ability that has taken Wigan to many victories this season.

Thank goodness Eric's not lost to the game altogether and I would like to take this opportunity of sincerely wishing him a long and successful coaching career.

BRIAN BATTY (Daily Mail).

Eric Ashton's decision to retire will cause a great deal of regret in Wigan as well as throughout the game after a wonderful career spanning almost 15 seasons. He has earned and enjoyed every possible honour and it is typical of his fine judgement that he doesn't want to dim the memory of those great days. I for one prefer to remember him in his finest hour. A tall, elegant figure commanding a game with intelligent kicking and demoralising a defence with his long striding breaks and perfectly timed passes. Ashton possessed the most admirable qualities as a player, proving the perfect gentleman and diplomat either on or off the field.

While Central Park mourns the end of another great era it is consolation to many that he remains in the game as Wigan's coach. Let us hope that he can lift Wigan back to the top under his inspired leadership.

187

ERIC ASHTON T

ST. HELENS XII
Blue Shirts, White Shorts

Full back
1 **K. GWILLIAM (Salford)**

Threequarters
2 **L. JONES (St. Helens)**
3 **W. BENYON (St. Helens**
4 **E. ASHTON (Wigan)**
5 **B. GLOVER (Warrington)**

Half backs
6 **A. MURPHY (Leigh)**
7 **T. BISHOP (St. Helens)**

Forwards
8 **D. CHISNALL (Leigh)**
9 **E. HUGHES (Widnes)**
10 **B. HOGAN (Wigan)**
11 **E. CHISNALL (St. Helen**
12 **R. FRENCH (Widnes)**
13 **G. FLETCHER (Oldham)**

Substitutes
14 **W. ASPINALL (Warringt**
15 **K. PARR (Warrington)**

Mr. C

Mr. J. ME

Mr. E. GL

...MONIAL MATCH

WIGAN XIII
Cherry and White Shirts, White Shorts

Full back
C. HESKETH (Salford)

Threequarters
W. J. BOSTON (Wigan)
W. ASHURST (Wigan)
J. MELLING (Warrington)
J. STOPFORD (Swinton)

Half backs
C. HILL (Wigan)
P. GORDON (Warrington)

Forwards
K. ASHCROFT (Wigan)
W. SAYER (St. Helens)
B. BRADY (Warrington)
G. LYON (Wigan)
K. O'LOUGHLIN (Wigan)
J. BRENNAN (Salford)

Substitutes
J. MOLYNEUX (Wigan)
K. MILLS (Wigan)

...AVIES
)

s
t. Helens)

K (Wigan)

189

Eric with the R.L. Challenge Cup after beating Workington Town at Wembley in 1958

ERIC THOMPSON (Lancashire Evening Post and Chronicle).

One little story I heard at Eastertime sums up the star with whom I'm proud to have been associated for over 14 seasons. A life-long St. Helens supporter decided to take his son to his first Rugby League game for the annual Wigan-St. Helens derby match. "This is the last chance you'll have to see a living legend before he finished playing" said the Saints fan.

Quite naturally he was as disappointed as any other St. Helens supporter about his team's defeat, but he turned to his son after a magnificent Eric Ashton display for Wigan and said, "You've got a memory now that will last all your life — a great player who comes from your hometown. I wanted you to see someone I've enjoyed for 14 years."

That lad, and thousands of others, have a final chance to put Eric Ashton in their memory album in the specially arranged tribute game at Central Park this Spring Bank holiday. And what memories Eric Ashton has left behind him.

The British captain whom Australian Chairman Bill Buckley termed the greatest ambassador England had ever sent to Australia; the Rivington Road schoolboy who became the first Rugby League player to be honoured by the Queen, with the M.B.E. has left his hallmark of class wherever he has played.

It would take a book to recount my memories of Eric Ashton, but the one which has left an indelible impression on me is that of the most genuine sportsman I have ever known — a player who has earned the respect of everyone who has played with or against him, and the thousands who have watched and known him. Eric Ashton earned everbody's respect.

191

Eric at the start of his career with Ernie Ashcroft

JACK WINSTANLEY (Wigan Observer).

Eric "The Grumbler" Ashton can rely on just three letters — M.B.E. — to make him remembered in unique fashion among all Rugby League players. But there is much more to this oustanding man than the fact that he is the only Rugby League player ever to receive a Royal accolade, memorable though that honour was.

Why do I call him "The Grumbler"? Simply because throughout my association with Eric Ashton he was always at his best when he was grumbling. But his discontent was based on a constant quest for improvement. And it's so often the disatisfied who make most progress. Certainly that could be said of Ashton — a man who, I believe, possesses the ability to have tackled and conquered many lucrative jobs outside Rugby League. Yet, thank goodness, he remained singlemindedly at Central Park to guide the club to unrivalled honours.

Like all other players, Eric Ashton has had his knockers, mainly because he had the wit to steer clear of unnecessary trouble and injury. It is well that he did, considering the occasions that the Wigan team has looked like a rudderless ship without him.

No man is indispensible, but Ashton came perilously close to being so on more than one occasion. In any event no Rugby League player who receives the Challenge Cup three times at Wembley and captains Great Britain both home and abroad does so without merit.

For much of his memorable career, Eric Ashton has played with great success the twin roles of architect and builder and history will

193

surely show that Wigan R.L.F.C. never made a more valuable signing. I cannot help wondering how many times the directors of his home town club, St. Helens, have regretted letting him slip through their fingers as a youngster and not paying the £15,000 fee when Ashton was on the transfer list for the only time.

As he himself will admit, Eric Ashton has been well paid for his services to Rugby League. The biggest tribute I can pay is to say that he has earned every halfpenny, and express the hope that his Testimonial match will bring him a handsome bonus.

JACK WOOD *former Wigan R.L. secretary, now secretary of Lancashire County Cricket Club.*

Eric Ashton can be summed up in one word — QUALITY. There is quality in everything he does and it is knowing men of such calibre that makes it so rewarding to be connected with the sporting world. I have never been so close to a sportsman as I was to Eric during my years at Central Park. He was, and is, one of my greatest friends.

Ashton's greatness as a player and a leader speaks for itself. I shall never forget the wonderful moments I shared with him after Wigan beat Workington at Wembley in 1958 — nor the sadder occasion when Wakefield beat us in 1963.

There could not possibly be a greater captain in Rugby League than Eric Ashton and now that his playing career is over I sincerely hope the Wigan directors will be wise enough to retain his services for as long as they possibly can.

Eric Ashton leading the Wigan team out at Wembley for the R.L.C.C. Final against Hull in 1959

Scoring one of his many tries, this being the Hull match on 14/9/68

Eric relaxing with his wife Doreen and daughters Michelle and Beverley

Printed by J. Starr & Sons Ltd., Dawber Street Works, Wigan

Glory In The Centre Spot

ERIC ASHTON'S
STATISTICAL CAREER SUMMARY
Compiled by Mike Latham

Wigan

	Apps	Subs	Tries	Goals	Points
1955/56	32	0	20	52	164
1956/57	41	0	18	95	244
1957/58	43	0	37	14	139
1958/59	32	0	16	0	48
1959/60	35	0	24	64	200
1960/61	28	0	20	14	88
1961/62	40	0	24	3	78
1962/63	32	0	11	45	123
1963/64	33	0	14	6	54
1964/65	40	1	10	13	56
1965/66	39	0	9	46	119
1966/67	29	4	8	44	112
1967/68	32	2	12	15	66
1968/69	31	3	8	37	98
TOTAL	487	10	231	448	1589

Great Britain

	Opponents	Venue	Res	T	G	
17/06/1957	Australia	Sydney	L 6-31	0	0	World Cup
25/06/1957	New Zealand	Sydney	L 21-29	0	0	World Cup
05/07/1958	Australia	Brisbane	W 25-18	0	0	
19/07/1958	Australia	Sydney	W 40-17	0	0	
26/07/1958	New Zealand	Auckland	L 10-15	0	0	
09/08/1958	New Zealand	Auckland	W 32-15	2	0	
14/03/1959	France	Leeds	W 50-15	1	0	
17/10/1959	Australia	Swinton	L 14-22	0	0	
21/11/1959	Australia	Leeds	W 11-10	0	0	
12/12/1959	Australia	Wigan	W 18-12	0	0	
06/03/1960	France	Toulouse	L 18-20	1	0	
26/03/1960	France	St Helens	D 17-17	0	0	
24/09/1960	New Zealand	Bradford	W 23-8	1	0	World Cup
08/10/1960	Australia	Bradford	W 10-3	0	0	World Cup
30/09/1961	New Zealand	Leeds	L 11-29	0	0	
21/10/1961	New Zealand	Bradford	W 23-10	1	0	
04/11/1961	New Zealand	Swinton	W 35-19	1	0	
17/02/1962	France	Wigan	L 15-20	1	0	
11/03/1962	France	Perpignan	L 13-23	1	0	
09/06/1962	Australia	Sydney	W 31-12	2	0	
30/06/1962	Australia	Brisbane	W 17-10	0	1	
14/07/1962	Australia	Sydney	L 17-18	1	0	
02/12/1962	France	Perpignan	L 12-17	1	0	
03/04/1963	France	Wigan	W 42-4	1	0	
16/10/1963	Australia	Wembley	L 2-28	0	0	
09/11/1963	Australia	Swinton	L 12-50	0	0	

Great Britain (non Tests)

10/10/1960	The Rest	Odsal	W 33-27	2	0	

England

17/11/1962	France	Leeds	W 18-6	1	0	

British XIII

	Opponents	Venue	Res	T	G
01/07/1957	Queensland	Brisbane	W 44-5	3	0
06/07/1957	France XIII	Auckland	W 26-12	2	0
20/07/1957	France XIII	Benoni, SA	W 61-41	2	0
24/07/1957	France XIII	Durban, SA	W 32-11	2	0
27/07/1957	France XIII	East London, SA	W 69-11	0	0

Northern Hemisphere

	Opponents	Venue	Res	T	G
08/07/1957	New Zealand	Auckland	W 34-31	5	5

Lancashire

12/10/1955	New Zealand	Warrington	L 15-17	0	0
16/09/1957	Cumberland	Workington	L 12-22	1	3
10/09/1958	Cumberland	Wigan	W 60-12	3	0
24/09/1958	Yorkshire	Hull KR	L 19-35	0	0
29/10/1958	Yorkshire	Leigh	L 15-16	1	0
23/09/1959	Australia	St Helens	W 30-22	2	0
11/11/1959	Yorkshire	Leigh	L 28-38	0	0
27/05/1961	Cumberland	Salford	W 32-18	0	0
13/09/1961	New Zealand	Warrington	W 15-13	0	0
18/09/1961	Cumberland	Workington	L 18-21	0	0

Great Britain Tours

		Apps	Sub	Tries	Goals
1958 Tour	excluding 4 Tests	15	0	28	13
1962 Tour	excluding 3 Tests	11	1	18	13

Tour Trial

12/03/1958	Whites v Greens	1	0	3	0

World Cup Trial

12/09/1960	GB v Rest of Lge	1	0	0	0

CAREER TOTAL		559	11	318	483

Career Honours

	Opponents	*Venue*	*Result*

Championship

21/05/1960	Wakefield	Odsal	W 27-3

Challenge Cup Finals

10/05/1958	Workington	Wembley	W 13-9
09/05/1959	Hull	Wembley	W 30-13
13/05/1961	St Helens	Wembley	L 6-12
11/05/1963	Wakefield	Wembley	L 10-25
08/05/1965	Hunslet	Wembley	W 20-16
21/05/1966	St Helens	Wembley	L 2-21

Lancashire Cup Finals

19/10/1957	Oldham	Swinton	L 8-13
29/10/1966	Oldham	Swinton	W 16-13

Floodlit Trophy Final

17/12/1968	St Helens	Wigan	W 7-4

Miscellaneous

Wigan debut

20/08/1955   Dewsbury   home

Wigan last game

03/05/1969   Salford   home

Wigan captaincy

from September 1957 onwards

Coaching career

	From	*To*
Wigan	Sep-63	May-73
Leeds	Jun-73	May-74
St Helens	May-74	May-80
Great Britain		Tour 1979
England	1978	1980

Directorships

St Helens   1982 to 2008

Chairmanship

St Helens   1993 to 1997

Awarded MBE

June 1966

Available now or coming soon from Scratching Shed Publishing Ltd...

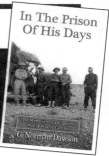

Scratching Shed Publishing Ltd

Scratching Shed Publishing Ltd is an independent publishing company founded in May 2008. We aim to produce high-quality books covering a wide range of subjects - including sport, travel and popular culture - of worldwide interest yet with the distinctive flavour of the North of England.

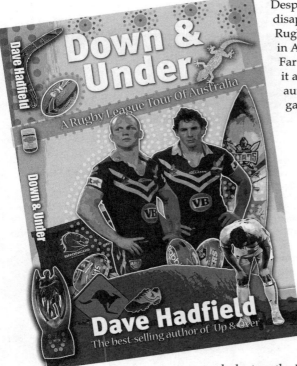